CW01501512

DEFENCE AND THE UK CONSTITUTION

First published by Haus Publishing in 2025
4 Cinnamon Row
London SW11 3TW
www.hauspublishing.com

Copyright © Nigel D. White, 2025

The right of the authors to be identified as the author of this work has been
asserted in accordance with the Copyright, Designs and Patents Act 1988

A CIP catalogue record for this book is
available from the British Library

Please note that no part of this book may be used or reproduced in any manner
for the purpose of training artificial intelligence technologies or systems

ISBN: 978-1-914979-21-7
eISBN: 978-1-914979-22-4

Typeset in Garamond by MacGuru Ltd

Printed in Czechia

The authorised representative in the EEA is:
Haus Publishing
Casella Postale 32
50037 San Piero a Sieve (Fi)
Italy
gpsr@hauspublishing.com

HAUS CURIOSITIES

DEFENCE AND THE UK CONSTITUTION

Nigel D. White

About the Author

NIGEL D. WHITE is emeritus professor of public international law at the University of Nottingham. His books include *Keeping the Peace*, *Democracy Goes to War*, and *Military Justice*.

Haus Curiosities

Inspired by the topical pamphlets of the interwar years, as well as by Einstein's advice to 'never lose a holy curiosity', Haus Publishing's Curiosities series presents short works of opinion and analysis by notable figures, under the guidance of the series editor, Peter Hennessy. Welcoming contributions from a diverse pool of authors since 2014, the series aims to reinstate the concise and incisive booklet as a powerful strand of politico-literary life, amplifying the voices of those who have something urgent to say about a topical theme.

The Constitution Society

The Constitution Society is an independent educational foundation. It works to promote public understanding of the UK constitution and to encourage informed debate between legislators, academics, and the public about proposals for constitutional change. The Society is a registered, entirely independent charity with no connection to any political party. For funding, the Society relies on individual donations and grants from educational trusts and foundations. You can learn more about the work of the Constitution Society at *www.consoc.org.uk*.

Contents

Framing Defence

The defence paradox

In this book I explore what can be called the paradox of defence in the UK constitution. This means that defence is at the heart of our country but often appears untrammelled by our constitution. There seems to be a lack of effective legal constraint and accountability for decisions that can affect the safety of millions.

The UK constitution lacks a single document called the 'constitution' and so is often described as 'unwritten' or uncodified. This is applauded by constitutional experts including A. V. Dicey, the most famous exponent of UK constitutional law, for its flexibility.[1] With it, or so the argument goes, we are able to adapt to new threats, including in the current era's remote, hybrid, and cyber warfare. Walter Bagehot, another classical and still-influential constitutional lawyer, defends this aspect of what he calls the 'efficient' part of the constitution, especially the fact that it allows the government to act 'in very dangerous times' by using a 'reserve of power fit for and needed by extreme exigencies'.[2]

Dicey and Bagehot both wrote their seminal works on

the British constitution back in the nineteenth century, but their portrayal of the constitution as adaptable, flexible, and enabling efficient executive action is equally applicable today. This is especially so in the areas of defence and security, despite the increase in the number of written laws specifically directed at national security.

The 'efficiency' of military and security operations, which is often combined with the need for 'secrecy', are claimed by political and military leaders, as well as the heads of the security services, as reasons for rapid decision-making and limited parliamentary and judicial oversight. I argue that these reasons are not sufficient. The impact of secrecy on defence is shown by the propensity of the government to deploy special forces (in particular the SAS) to conflicts around the world with maximum secrecy on the basis that any publicity would undermine the effectiveness of the operation and the safety of special forces personnel. However, such an approach prevents effective democratic accountability. And even when there is accountability, secrecy is still the predominant concern.[3]

The decisions and actions taken in the name of defending the realm or in pursuit of national security can lead to the invasion of another country, the killing of unarmed protestors, drone strikes against individuals, the preventive detention, rendition, or indeed killing of suspected terrorists, or the withdrawal of citizenship.[4] Historically, it seems some of these decisions have been taken to the detriment of citizens or individuals both within the UK and those subject to its control overseas, often with very little accountability. It is important we understand why, and how this type of decision-making persists within our constitution.

In *Defence and the UK Constitution*, I want to explore the nature and extent of the defence paradox. I do this through a distinction drawn between the 'legal constitution' (discussed in Chapter 2) and the 'political constitution' of the UK (covered in Chapter 3). This contrasts the bodies, statutes, rules, and precedents governing defence (the legal), with those discretionary (executive, prerogative, statutory, and conventional) powers (the political) that have empowered governments to act in ways that sometimes appear to fly in the face of constitutionalism and flout the rule of law. In the final chapter, I frame defence within the international constitutional order, where the UK has rights and duties arising from a complex web of bilateral and multilateral commitments. With this covered, I ask whether defence can sit comfortably within our constitution. Simply put: can our defence be brought under stronger constitutional restraint without undermining its ability to deliver security for the UK?

Of national and international constitutions

Before we can understand whether executive decisions and actions in the areas of defence and security are lawful under the UK constitution, or are abuses of power and unconstitutional, we need to start to with a basic understanding of what our 'constitution' entails. It has been suggested, albeit controversially, in the *Thoburn* (metric measures) case of 2002, that there is a distinction to be drawn between pieces of legislation that can be construed as constitutional – those that regulate the relationship between state and citizen or impact on fundamental rights – and ordinary statutes. The argument goes that the latter can be repealed by later inconsistent statutes, the former can only be repealed with the express intent of Parliament.[5] Despite this suggestion of a constitutional hierarchy in the UK, there is no written constitution which might formalise such a view.

I understand 'constitution' in the sense given by the House of Lords Committee on the Constitution in 2001 as: 'the set of laws, rules and practices that create the basic institutions of the state ... and stipulate the powers of those institutions and the relationship between the different institutions and between those institutions and the individual'.[6] This definition, which focuses on the legal powers of the various organs of the state and the legal relationship between the state and the individual, should be kept in mind when considering the constitutionality of defence.

However, this definition fails to capture the wider values of society that underpin the constitution: values of peace and security, but also of liberty and the rule of law. Defence could be understood broadly to include defence of those values, but care must be taken not to elevate 'defence' and 'security' above all values, as that would lead to an Orwellian 'Big Brother' state. Interestingly, in a key government defence and security strategy document of 2021, the UK's 'interests' were said to be 'sovereignty', 'security', and 'prosperity', while its 'shared values' were stated to be 'universal human rights, the rule of law, free speech and fairness and equality'.[7] Differences aside, such depictions and claims about what underpins our polity provide the broader context within which debates about the UK's constitution are conducted.

Furthermore, there are constitutional peculiarities somewhat hidden in the Committee's definition. Of most relevance for our purposes are the continuing role of both non-statutory prerogative powers and non-binding conventions. They sit uneasily with the idea of a constitution as a legal framework for containing and regulating political discretion. Prerogative powers are derived from powers formerly in the hands of the monarch. They are non-statutory powers exercised on behalf of the state (traditionally known as 'the Crown') by ministers. Historically, they do not require the approval of Parliament when they are used. Dicey's description should raise concerns: 'the prerogative appears to be both historically and as a matter of actual fact nothing else than the residue of discretionary or arbitrary authority, which at any given time is legally left in the hands of the Crown'.[8]

Further concerns are raised when considering the important role of 'conventions' in the constitution. Dicey defined UK constitutional law as 'all rules which directly or indirectly affect the distribution or exercise of the sovereign power of the state'. He used the term 'rules' rather than 'laws' because the constitution consists of two types of rules. The first set are laws found in statutes and common law precedents which are enforceable by the courts, and the second are non-binding conventions 'which, though they may regulate the conduct ... of the sovereign power ... are not in reality laws at all since they are not enforced by the courts'.[9]

A combination of discretionary prerogative powers and non-legally binding conventions in the area of defence should raise alarm bells, at least if we expect to see legal restraints on the exercise of the physical might of the state. But when the government decides to send troops into combat, under the constitution these 'war powers' are exercised under the prerogative and are only limited by an uncertain non-binding convention that Parliament debate the issue beforehand. This convention was said to have been first established when the UK supported the US invasion of Iraq in 2003, and the House of Commons voted to support that action.[10] This shows that there is very little room for constitutional law as a restraint on power in this key aspect of defence. It is also evidence of the 'political' aspect of the constitution in the sense that such decisions are made on political rather than legal grounds and are subject to political and not judicial mechanisms of accountability.

Peace, security, and defence are not just values within the UK's constitutional order; they are pivotal in the international legal order governing relations between sovereign states. The institutional constitutional framework in matters of defence and security revolves around the United Nations (UN) Charter 1945 and other seminal treaties such as the North Atlantic Treaty 1948 (the founding document of NATO) and the Nuclear Non-Proliferation Treaty (NPT) of 1968 (said to be the 'grand bargain' on nuclear weapons).

In line with the practice of many sovereign states, the UK has developed a significant defence capability in terms of conventional military forces, but unlike most other states the UK's armoury includes nuclear weapons. It may seem incredible, when considering that we know about their existentially catastrophic nature, that the possession of nuclear weapons is not prohibited by international law. Chemical weapons are prohibited, but not nuclear weapons.[11] Indeed, the UK is a recognised 'nuclear-weapon state' under the NPT of 1968, and as such it has privileges belonging to only five states that had developed nuclear weapons by 1968 (US, Soviet Union, UK, France, and China). Those states, unlike any other, have the legal right to possess such weapons while committing to a longer-term process of nuclear disarmament.

The UK's status as a recognised nuclear-weapon state means that it also has responsibilities to prevent nuclear war. These responsibilities may well be more political than legal. The doctrine of deterrence, which has justified the nuclear status quo since the US and Soviet

Union began a nuclear arms race in the 1950s, is largely a political doctrine premised on the mutually assured destruction (MAD) of those states engaged in nuclear war. Clearly this is a very precarious basis for peace.

It can be argued that MAD is compatible with the legal right of self-defence since the promise is to respond instantly to any nuclear attack with a devastating response in kind. The idea is that any state using nuclear weapons will itself be annihilated by an instant response in kind. However, the threatened state has very little time in which to launch its weapons before it is destroyed. This means that there is a real possibility of a nuclear weapons state using its weapons first in the belief that it is (or will imminently be) under attack by another such state. Imagine gunslingers in a Western movie armed with nuclear weapons rather than six-shooters – both are looking for that first move before using their weapon in a justified act of self-defence, so any twitch, real or imagined, can trigger an exchange of fire.

The UK constantly restates its faith in the doctrine of deterrence and, with it, the continued possession of nuclear weapons, particularly when justifying the upgrading of its submarine-based nuclear deterrent. In 2024, Sir Keir Starmer, the new Labour prime minister, stated that 'a strong, modernised nuclear capability is not just a pillar of our national defence – it's a cornerstone of our commitment to NATO and global security'.[12]

The same five states that are recognised nuclear-weapon states under the NPT 1968 are also the permanent members of the UN Security Council (known as the P5), a status that again confers privileges as well as responsibilities on those states. As a member of the P5, the UK has special privileges, particularly the right of veto over proposed decisions that might seek solutions to conflicts, impose economic sanctions, or authorise military measures to tackle threats to international peace and security.

The UK also shares responsibility for delivering the first purpose of the United Nations – the maintenance of international peace and security. Although politically, economically, and, indeed, militarily, the UK is no longer a great power, it still holds on to the legal trappings of such a state within the international constitutional order, and this has a significant impact on UK constitutional laws and practices. It can be seen too that the international constitution is, like its national counterpart in the UK, similarly a mixture of the political and the legal.

The international legal order was traditionally concerned with relations between sovereign states. However, after 1945 there has been the steady growth in treaties whose focus is to protect individual rights and freedoms from encroachment by the state. Sometimes those treaties create courts to oversee the enforcement of the state's duties, including to protect human rights. Particularly after the adoption of the European Convention on Human Rights (ECHR) 1950 and the creation of the European Court of Human Rights (ECtHR), the pendulum has started to swing towards the legal regulation of governmental power. Inevitably this has implications for the national constitutional order of the UK, where we see that human rights law has encroached upon the government's powers in defence and security. It goes without saying that this has led to political pushback.[13]

From defence to security

Having outlined an understanding of 'constitution', and glimpsing its multi-dimensional complexity, we turn to 'defence', which is no less difficult a concept given that 'defence' is understood much more broadly than just 'self-defence'. Nevertheless, self-defence is a solid basis upon which to start to build a legal understanding of defence.

Self-defence is seen as an inherent right. In national legal systems the right of persons to defend themselves from attack is one of the few exceptions to the government's monopoly on the use of force. In international law, self-defence is stated to be an inherent right of a state in the UN Charter of 1945 and is the only exception to the Security Council's monopoly. In other words, self-defence could be said to be a fundamental right which is embodied in both national and international legal orders. Indeed, according to de Vattel's late-eighteenth-century classic commentary, 'self-defence against an unjust attack is not only a right which every nation has, but it is a duty, and one of its most sacred duties'.[14]

However, 'defence' in the UK constitution is more

broadly understood than the right of 'self-defence' of the individual and the state in the face of an external attack. While the police, security services, and soldiers are largely confined to using potentially lethal force in self-defence or in defence of others in peacetime, they may not be so confined in times of war, armed conflicts, riots, or other states of emergency. More broadly, in order to preserve sovereign statehood, the sovereign or, in modern terms, the government has to be able to defend the state from external aggression and threats, but also as importantly to prevent violent disorder or threats from within.

A state's ability to defend and secure itself internally and externally is premised on it having gained a monopoly over the use of force within its borders, through its control and direction of the armed forces, security services, and police. In addition to being the most powerful force internally, the state's forces must be sufficient to deter and repel external aggressors. The exercise of sovereign power depends upon that monopoly on the use of force being maintained and challenges to it being met and defeated or at least suppressed to acceptable levels. This may take the form of military action within the UK, as in the period known as the 'Troubles' in Northern Ireland (1968–98), and military actions overseas to defend territory, as shown by the Falklands War of 1982. More controversially, it may take the form of offensive military action against sovereign states who are deemed to threaten the UK's national security, as was the case with the invasion and occupation of Iraq in 2003.

The broadly stated priorities of the Ministry of Defence (MoD) reflect both a colonial legacy and more modern concerns over both defence and security, namely to: protect the UK, its Crown dependencies, and overseas territories; pursue a campaigning approach to counter threats from states and non-state actors; promote the country's national interests globally; and secure strategic advantage, achieve greater economic and industrial resilience, and contribute to national prosperity.[15]

I feel it is important to consider defence in the broad sense, to include defence and security. This widens my analysis to include internal and external threats, the security services as well as the armed forces. This accords with the trend towards 'national security' replacing, to a degree, 'defence of the realm' in legal and political discourse. According to Lord Diplock in a leading case on the use of prerogative powers in the field of national security (the *GCHQ* case of 1985), this trend is due to the use of national security terminology in the ECHR.[16]

Defence is at the core of the UK as a sovereign state, not just as a basic function but as an essential element of the state. According to the courts, 'There is a duty on the King, by reason of his being King, to defend the realm, and therefore of course all of his realm and every part of his realm'.[17] Without being able to defend and secure the realm, the UK would be compromised as a sovereign, independent state. Defence is fundamental. The argument I make is that it also needs to be constitutional.

Constitutionalism and the rule of law

Constitutionalism aims to restrict the power of the state, specifically the executive or government, through the restraint of such power by constitutional rules, as well as by political and legal institutions that can provide checks on the use and abuse of power by the executive.

In this regard, the Magna Carta or Great Charter of 1215, which for many remains the foundation stone of the modern British constitution, divides opinion. On the one hand it has been dismissed as 'an ancient fetish, a sort of medicine bag, pulled out of the dust of the record-room ... and made into the symbol of the struggle against arbitrary power'. It follows from this line of reasoning that 'the true effect of the Charter, if any, had been merely the hardening of the privileges of some hundred petty kings'.[18] On the other hand, for many the Charter is the source of our liberties, the beginnings of constitutionalism and the establishment of the rule of law over the monarch. Whichever view one takes, though, it is clear that the Charter did mark a pivotal point in British history away from exclusive rule by the monarch, towards rule by the state of which the monarch was but one part.

However, rule by the state does not imply the rule of law. The constitutional order of the state may still permit the significant use of arbitrary political power. In particular, the state has a natural tendency to preserve this for itself in defence and security. Nonetheless, Dicey would contend that the British constitution is based on the rule of law, meaning 'the absolute supremacy or predominance of regular laws as opposed to the influence of arbitrary power'.[19] But we should not place too much reliance on the rule of law. It is not, by itself, the remedy for arbitrary power. A government, elected with a large majority, can push legislation through a compliant Parliament thereby giving itself wide discretionary and possibly arbitrary powers under statute.

The point is that such arbitrary power is not just found in those 'residual' privileges deriving from monarchs and which is now in the hands of government ministers – so called 'prerogative' powers, in particular the power to deploy troops to armed conflicts overseas and to confront national emergencies at home. Arbitrary power can also be found in legislation which grants wide-ranging executive powers that infringe the rights of individuals. In recent times, examples would include the Terrorism Act 2000, Civil Contingencies Act 2004, Coronavirus Act 2020, and the National Security Act 2023. These statutes were adopted as a response to new threats and emergencies, with national security being the justification for each extra grab of executive power by the government. Embodying such discretionary powers in statutes might provide the veneer of legality, but it is long way from the idea of constitutionalism – meaning that law places restraints on such state power.

The weaknesses in both the rule of law and constitutionalism in the UK is partly explained by the predominance of politics over law at the level of state and government. In a lecture on the 'political constitution' given in 1979, J. A. G. Griffith declared that 'the constitution lives on, changing from day to day for the constitution is no more and no less than what happens'.[20] In matters of defence and security, there is judicial support for such a notion. In the *Gentle* case of 2008, the House of Lords dismissed claims made by the mothers of two British soldiers who had lost their lives in Iraq in 2003–4 fighting what they argued was an illegal war. The Court declared that the legality of the war was a matter of 'political judgment', which was not the proper subject of judicial review.[21]

2

The Legal Constitution

Defence of the realm and national security

In the first chapter we established that defence within the constitution covers both defence of the realm and national security. In this chapter, I first examine the changing, and sometimes troubled, position of defence within the constitution by tracing its role in the social contract between the state and the people.

I then identify the key public bodies and organs that form the defence and security establishment of the UK today. In more general terms, while these various bodies, organs, and committees often predated the emerging statutory framework for defence and security, they have subsequently become entwined in these legal frameworks. This is emblematic of the way the British constitution has evolved. However, in the areas of defence and national security, I show that it has far-reaching consequences for the social contract underpinning the UK, as well as for the role of the courts in asserting legal limits to political discretion.

Defence and the social contract

Defence occupied a troubled position in the emerging British state. This is reflected in constitutional documents adopted at key points in our history. The Petition of Right 1628 was essentially a protest against arbitrary imprisonment but also against the military's role in the state through the use of commissions of martial law in times of peace, and the housing of soldiers in privately owned property. However, as with many of these ancient documents, the grand claims to rights were limited by the powers of the Crown: 'the King yielded' to the claims in the Petition of Right 'though the effect of the concession was weakened by the view Charles I held that his prerogative powers were not thereby diminished'.[1]

Fears of the development of a standing army which might threaten Parliament led to the Bill of Rights 1689. This limited the power of the monarch and subjected the armed forces to renewal by Parliament. In tandem, the Mutiny Act 1689 subjected the military not only to the criminal law of the land but also to specific military offences. Seventeenth-century legislation may seem irrelevant in today's world. However, it's still the case that Parliament has to renew the mandate of the armed forces on a regular basis, and the codification of military law today in fact builds on the Mutiny Act 1689. Fastforward, and the Armed Forces Act 2006 rationalised the separate system of military justice that governs the armed forces. The reality is that parliamentary control of the military still revolves around its power to adopt these pieces of legislation, without which the military would have no legal basis in the UK.

Such legislation develops and adjusts the social contract underpinning the basic law of constitution of the UK – the Magna Carta 1215, which sought to establish a more secure kingdom through balancing the power between monarch and barons, and by removing foreign forces, especially mercenaries, from the land. Although the Charter's contents have limited constitutional relevance in the UK today, its importance as a crude social contract should not be underestimated. It established in law the right of the 'state' to exercise power over the people in return for providing security and upholding limited rights.

In times of insecurity, that contract may be revised in favour of the state, while in times of peace and prosperity the balance may swing towards the individual in terms of greater freedoms and rights. But security is not the only factor which might cause a change. Agitation for greater representation, greater democracy or sovereignty, can also drive significant constitutional change. The supremacy of Parliament in the UK means that it can alter the constitution by statute;[2] in fact, a significant piece of legislation is likely to shift the constitution, however marginally, either in favour of the state or the individual.

The expansion of the power of the state and the constriction of civil liberties of the individual are clearly shown during the two world wars. The Defence of the

Realm Act 1914 included provisions for detention without trial of persons of 'hostile origin or associations'. The judiciary upheld the validity of such detentions, declaring that 'it may be necessary in time of great public danger to entrust great powers' to the government, reassuringly adding 'that Parliament may do so feeling certain that such powers will be reasonably exercised'.[3] In 1939, Parliament passed the Emergency Powers (Defence) Act under which the government asked for and was given powers to 'make such Regulations ... as appear necessary or expedient for securing the public safety, the defence of the realm, the maintenance of public order and the efficient prosecution of any war in which His Majesty may be engaged'. Regulations again permitted detention without trial for those reasonably believed to be of hostile intent or involved in 'acts prejudicial to the public safety or the defence of the realm', a power which again was accepted as necessary by the courts.[4]

The freedoms of citizens were further restricted in pursuit of defence during the world wars by the conscription of adult males to the armed forces, something which only operated in the UK in 1916–18 (Military Service Act 1916) and 1939–60 (National Service (Armed Forces) Act 1939 and National Service Act 1948). National service was continued after the Second World War because of the manpower needed to administer occupied countries, particularly Germany (1945–55), and to tackle violent emergencies in the increasingly unstable empire, for example in Malaya (1948–60), Cyprus (1955–9) and Kenya (1952–60). The growing threat from the Soviet Union also led to pressure to maintain significant military forces to deter Soviet aggression.[5] Conscripts fought alongside regular British soldiers against North Korean and Chinese soldiers in the brutal Korean War (1950–53).

In 1946, Prime Minister Attlee defended the extension of conscription for 'training for citizenship as well as defence'. He denied that national service was undemocratic: 'we are steadily increasing the rights of citizens in this country … the more rights we can give our people, the better; but rights involve obligations'.[6] Nonetheless, unrest in the ranks of conscripts in far-flung colonial outposts in the late 1940s – where the living conditions of soldiers were often appalling – grew but was met with the full force of military justice, with courts martial for mutiny and other military offences occurring regularly.[7] More recently, a proposal for national service re-emerged during the general-election campaign of 2024, alongside more extreme suggestions by Sir Patrick Sanders, chief of the general staff, for the need of a citizen army in the face of the growing threat from Russia following its invasion and ongoing war with Ukraine.[8]

Across time, the government responds to major threats to security by adjusting the social contract underpinning the state so that the balance shifts towards security and away from liberty. It can do this by using its majority in Parliament and by the fact that the opposition parties are often unlikely to challenge changes driven by arguments of national security or defence of the realm. Thus, although we remain within a legal constitution in the area of defence, we are never wholly distant from the state's predilection to limit certain basic civil liberties.

The organisation of defence

According to the Ministry of Defence the 'defence purpose' is 'to protect the people of the United Kingdom, prevent conflict, and be ready to fight our enemies'.[9] A unified MoD was established as a government department in its modern form in 1964, prior to which there were a number of separate ministries, including the Admiralty, War Office, and Air Ministry.

In 1964, the armed services: the Army, Royal Navy, and Royal Air Force (with a current combined strength of around 180,000 service personnel) were all brought within the organisational framework of the MoD. The MoD has a dual role in formulating defence and national security policies and plans and in generating military capability and delivering its use. On the operational side, the Military Strategic Headquarters directs and carries out military operations on behalf of the government.

On the policy side the MoD renews the UK defence strategy every five years or so to reflect the government's priorities as well as to adjust to emerging threats. In 2021, the strategy identified the problems thrown up by the technological transformation of security threats and warfare, which have led to 'our adversaries' undermining 'the international norms and values that have underpinned our security and our prosperity'. In response the MoD is developing a range of non-lethal as well as lethal responses to an increasingly diverse set of threats, from cyber-attacks to full-scale invasions.[10] By identifying state threats from China, North Korea, and Iran as well as Russia, defence of the UK can involve operations all over the world, stretching the UK's armed forces very thinly. This over-reach has characterised British military commitments in the recent past – in Afghanistan and Iraq. This is nothing new, though. Max Hastings, a leading military historian, has argued that 'throughout its history, Britain has repeatedly sought to ignore the importance of mass on the battlefield, despatching inadequate forces to assert moral or strategic principles'.[11]

The MoD is headed by the secretary of state for defence (defence secretary), one of the principal secretaries of state appointed by the prime minister. The defence secretary is a member of the Cabinet, which is the ultimate government decision-making body. According to the MoD the 'Defence Secretary's powers to act come from Parliamentary legislation (for example the Armed Forces Acts) and the common law, as well as from the Royal Prerogative, both as a senior member of the government and as the Chair of the Defence Council'.[12] The Defence Council provides legal cover for the numerous other boards and committees in the MoD. Having said that, the Council's powers derive from an opaquer source, namely 'letters patent' granted under prerogative in 1964. Essentially, this amounted to the government giving powers to the defence secretary to command and administer the armed forces. In addition to the defence secretary, the Defence Council includes other ministers (for example for defence procurement) and military chiefs of staff.

The influence of the chiefs of staff upon the development of defence has been considerable. For instance, in response to the discovery in 1954 that the Soviet Union had exploded a hydrogen bomb fifty times more powerful than the atomic weapon, chiefs of staff recommended that the UK should develop its own thermonuclear weapons to act as a deterrent to replace the atomic weapons first tested by the UK in 1952. That recommendation was accepted by ministers in 1954,[13] and Britain's first thermonuclear device ('Yellow Sun') was tested off Christmas Island in 1957. Although nuclear weapons are part of the military arsenal of the UK, control of them is political, ultimately in the hands of the prime minister possibly meeting for advice in the National Security Council (Nuclear), a Cabinet committee which considers nuclear deterrence and nuclear security.

Though not always explicit, the constitutional arrangement of both defence and security hinges upon the control of the military and defence establishment by the government – the defence secretary and, ultimately, the prime minister. You might reasonably expect control to be watertight in the case of the ultimate weapon. There is, however, the issue of how the UK's small nuclear arsenal operates within the much more potent US nuclear deterrent. The UK's decision to have a submarine-based nuclear deterrent was made in the early 1960s after the US agreed to supply Polaris missiles to which British warheads were fitted. President Kennedy hoped to completely bind the UK's nuclear arsenal to the US by these means, but Prime Minister Harold Macmillan 'secured a let-out' that recognised that the UK's nuclear deterrent would be used 'for the international defence of the Western Alliance in all circumstances except where Her Majesty's Government may decide that the supreme national interests are at stake'.[14] This is apparently sufficient to enable the MoD to state that 'decision making and use of' nuclear weapons 'remains entirely sovereign to the UK; only the Prime Minister can authorise the launch of nuclear weapons, which ensures that political control is maintained at all times'.[15]

However, the MoD's confident assertion is not only undermined by the uneven and opaque relationship with the US, but also by the fact that, in the event of nuclear war, submarine commanders may have to take the initiative. This is reflected in sealed 'letters of last resort' given to the commanders of the four UK nuclear submarines by the prime minister. These letters are said to give discretion to commanders to initiate nuclear retaliation themselves if they are unable to make contact with the government. The doomsday scenario behind these instructions is that the UK has been attacked by nuclear weapons and its infrastructure destroyed. Despite this catastrophic scenario, the thinking is that the UK's nuclear deterrent can still be delivered from out at sea by the submarine commanders exercising what might be termed the ultimate discretion – to launch arguably futile retaliatory nuclear strikes at enemy cities, causing hundreds of thousands of deaths. Or, you might argue, this is MAD taken to its logical conclusion.

Apart from the conduct of military operations, the everyday running of the MoD and armed forces is delegated to the Defence Board, which is also chaired by the defence secretary. The Defence Board has responsibility for delivering the 'Defence Vision', which is put in hubristic terms by the MoD on its website: 'to defend the United Kingdom and its interests, strengthen international peace and stability, and act as a force for good in the world'. The MoD, then, is not only tasked with the defence of the realm, but it also has to be ready to undertake expeditionary operations overseas to help secure international peace and broader visions of what is good for the world. The propensity to try to do 'good' through forceful means is reflected in British military interventions to protect civilians in Kosovo in 1999 and Libya in 2011. These actions initially worked, although longer-term liberal interventions to install democracies in these and other countries – Afghanistan and Iraq – failed miserably.

The organisation of security

The three security and intelligence services are the Security Service (MI5), the Secret Intelligence Service

(MI6), and Government Communications Head-quarters (GCHQ). MI5's mission is to keep the country safe, including from terrorism, espionage, and sabotage. MI6 addresses the external aspect of national security – it acts secretly around the world to address threats to the UK including terrorism, activities of hostile states, and cyber threats. GCHQ provides government and operational bodies such as the military, security services, and the police with information gained through monitoring, collecting, and analysing data and communications that are deemed to have intelligence value.

A statutory framework for the security services is a relatively recent development, coming with the enactment of the Security Service Act 1989 and the Intelligence Services Act 1994, even though MI5 and MI6 can be traced back to 1909. MI5 has been described by the courts as being established under prerogative powers,[16] although 'no convincing authority was cited for such an assertion'.[17] The MI6 website suggests that 'although our work is secret, everything we do is legal and underpinned by the values that define the UK'. Although this claim is stronger after 1994 when the agency was put on a statutory footing, it is worth noting that section 7 of that Act gives the secretary of state the power to authorise acts by MI6 agents outside the UK which would be unlawful if committed in the UK. Practice under this so-called 'James Bond clause', including instances of potentially lethal force being used by British agents, is predictably clouded in secrecy with limited accountability. Who controls the security services is also not always clear. According to the courts, for instance, no ministerial authorisation was necessary when GCHQ shared information with the CIA about a foreign national, leading to their death along with others by a US drone strike in Pakistan in 2011, nor did any criminal liability attach to GCHQ.[18]

The presence of US security services within the UK's security architecture also raises concerns. The UK's Joint Intelligence Committee (JIC) brings together the main 'producers' of intelligence (MI5, MI6, GCHQ, and Defence Intelligence) and the 'users' of such (MoD, FCDO, Home Office, and Treasury) and representatives of the intelligence agencies of Canada, New Zealand, and Australia where necessary. In contrast, the CIA's London chief attends every weekly meeting of the JIC. JIC assessments on matters of greatest concern will then inform government action. Infamously, this included the so-called 'dodgy dossier' on Iraq's WMD of 2002, which was allegedly 'sexed-up' to bolster the case for military intervention in Iraq. The dossier and events surrounding it, including the suicide of Dr David Kelly, a former UN weapons inspector, were the subject of two inquiries by Lord Hutton and Lord Butler, both of which largely exonerated the government.[19]

The institutional architecture of defence and security also includes Cabinet committees with significant policy and practical impact. Of these, the National Security Council (NSC), chaired by the prime minister, stands out as the forum where strategies are developed covering national security, foreign policy, resilience, international relations, economic security, trade, development, defence, and global issues. On a practical level COBRA (shorthand for the Civil Contingencies Committee) is another Cabinet committee that can be chaired by the prime minister, providing for high-level decision-making and coordination of the various emergency services in the event of national emergencies such as natural or man-made disasters, terrorist attacks, or major industrial disruption. The executive power of the prime minister in pulling together the coercive power of the state is facilitated through these committees.

Security, surveillance, and counter-terrorism

In contrast to the armed forces, which have been governed by statute since the first Mutiny Act 1689, a statutory framework for the security services was not put in place until the Interception of Communications Act 1985, the Security Service Act 1989, and the Intelligence Services Act 1994. This late change occurred because of the influence of the ECHR, which forced 'the UK to give to the security and intelligences agencies ... and to practices of interception a more solid legal base than they had previously enjoyed'.[20]

The creation of a statutory infrastructure surrounding national security would appear to be a positive legal development; indeed it has been described as the 'emergence of a national security constitution'.[21] However, as leading constitutional lawyers point out, despite the improvements in 'transparency, accountability and legality' in the area of security, there is evidence of the security and intelligence services continuing to stray beyond the statutory framework.[22] One glaring example is the involvement of British security agents in the improper treatment and rendition of detainees during the 'war on terror', examined inconclusively in a number of cases before UK courts[23] and subject to more critical review in an inquiry led by Sir Peter Gibson.[24]

Although there have been significant moves towards legislative backing for the security services, this by itself does not mean we have strengthened legality in this area. It could be argued that the turn to statute is evidence of governments becoming more emboldened in bringing the security services out of the shadows, at least to an extent that such legislation reinforces the public's faith in them. To allow a little light to shine on these agencies gives them legitimacy and feeds the public's romantic image of the secret service. It must be borne in mind that the overall effect of legislation is to empower the state (and its agencies) and only weakly to constrain it. The net result is an increase in the lawful range of investigatory and surveillance powers in the hands of the state's security services at the expense of the liberty enjoyed by persons. In a formal sense this satisfies the ECHR, which allows for the state to exercise powers to interfere with the exercise of human rights when it is necessary in the interests of national security, as long as those powers are exercised in accordance with the law.

Counter-terrorism laws give wide-ranging powers to the security services, allowing them to interfere extensively with the liberty of individuals. Indeed, they are often stated to be 'exceptional' powers.[25] Despite their exceptional nature, though, consensus now seems to be that the country needs a permanent set of counter-terrorism laws in addition to the existing criminal law. A clue as to why the exceptional nature of terrorism has become a permanent feature in the UK constitution can be found in the extremely broad definition of terrorism in s.1 of the Terrorism Act 2000. According to s.1, terrorism is an action such as serious violence against a person or serious damage to property 'designed to influence the government' or an international organisation 'or to intimidate the public', and 'is made for the purpose of advancing a political, religious, racial or ideological cause'.

The purpose of this provision is not to define a new crime of terrorism, since most terrorist offences violate existing criminal laws. Rather, the definition in s.1 acts as a trigger for the use of other counter-terrorism measures. For example, membership of a proscribed terrorist organisation is a criminal offence, and the Act also allows for extended pre-charge detention as well as granting powers of arrest in cases of suspected terrorism.

Terrorist funds are also targeted in the 2000 Act, powers enhanced when a suspected terrorist is listed by the UN Security Council and subject to targeted sanctions, which are incorporated into UK law by means of the United Nations Act 1946. These measures, including the freezing of assets and restrictions on the movement of targeted individuals were condemned by the Supreme Court in the *Ahmed* case as 'draconian', effectively making those targeted 'prisoners of state'.[26] The court quashed the order. However, this judgment was effectively nullified by Parliament adopting the Terrorist Asset Freezing (Temporary Provisions) Act 2010.

The definition of terrorism in the 2000 Act serves wider purposes too, though, in that it allows police and prosecutors to determine whether violent ideologically driven criminal conduct that has impact on the public or government should be prosecuted as a terrorist crime or an ordinary crime. Furthermore, that decision might be driven by political as well as legal concerns such as the need to demonstrate that there is an ongoing terrorist threat, which justifies the continuation of a state of exception. This in turn results in pressure for an ever-widening definition of terrorism.

It is the threat to the state (either the government or the public or both) by ideologically driven violence that makes terrorism exceptional. In simple terms, while ordinary crimes affect the individual, terrorist crimes impact the collective, including the state itself. This is demonstrated by the further widening of the definition by a series of qualifying provisions in the 2000 Act. For a start, there is no need to prove that the action is designed to influence government or intimidate the public if it involves the use of firearms or explosives. The other qualifying provisions effectively broaden the geographic scope of the definition of terrorist threats to include foreign governments. In *Gul*, the UK Supreme Court was critical of the 'very far reaching' definition of terrorism in the 2000 Act, which might, for example, cover the activities of victims of oppression in other countries. Disappointingly, the Court was not prepared to cut down the 'natural, very wide, meaning of the definition' of terrorism in the Act.[27]

Judicial deference to the national security powers of the executive were further evidenced in 2016. In *Miranda*, the Court of Appeal felt that the powers to stop and detain individuals suspected of terrorist actions contained in the Terrorism Act 2000 were properly used by police to stop the partner of a journalist and seize the files he was carrying. These files contained data stolen by Edward Snowden from the US National Security Agency. On the facts of the case the Court found that compelling national security arguments outweighed Mr Miranda's right under Article 10 ECHR to freedom of expression. However, it also found that the power was not sufficiently proscribed by law so as to avoid the risk that it would be exercised arbitrarily. However, the Court left it to Parliament to decide what safeguards would be needed to make that power compatible with the ECHR.[28]

In *Miranda,* the Court was making the point that although anti-terrorist powers may be given a statutory basis and, therefore, on one level appear to be compliant with the rule of law, they can be too broad so as to give those exercising such powers effectively unregulated power over individuals suspected of involvement in terrorism as broadly defined. It is a pity the UK Supreme Court in *Gul*, though expressing concern about the impact of the Act on the rule of law, did not make this very point in relation to the definition of terrorism itself, which as we have seen can trigger executive actions that strike at the heart of individual freedoms.

The definition of terrorism in the 2000 Act is even more remarkable given that it was adopted before the occurrence of what is considered the pivotal act of international terrorism – the attacks by al-Qaeda on the United States of 11 September 2001 (9/11). The 2000 Act arose from the need to replace the panoply of legislation designed to counter the terrorist threat in Northern Ireland, which had been much reduced following the Good Friday Accords of 1998, and anticipated the rise of Islamic, global terrorism.

After 9/11, the government's first instinct was to declare a state of emergency and empower police to detain suspected terrorists by enacting the Anti-Terrorism, Crime and Security Act 2001. In this the government formally departed from Article 5 of the ECHR, which guarantees the right to liberty and security, to enable the state to detain a number of foreign-born suspected terrorists. Departures (formally known as derogations) from some of the rights in the ECHR are allowed when there is an emergency threatening the life of the nation.

In the *Belmarsh* case, the court agreed that the

government's departure from Article 5 was permitted, but it found that the measures were disproportionate in that they unjustifiably discriminated against non-nationals.[29] In effect, rights and freedoms can be restricted in times of emergency but there are limits on the government's powers. It may be argued that the courts, in these cases, were too willing to accept the existence of a state of emergency threatening the 'life of the nation', when arguably there was no such threat to the UK. National security, however, is an argument that the courts are often not willing to tackle head-on, though they may try to curb any excessive use of executive power.

Judicial criticisms of the indefinite detention regime led to its replacement by control orders in the Prevention of Terrorism Act 2005. Such orders imposed obligations on targeted individuals 'for purposes connected with protecting members of the public from a risk of terrorism'. In some cases, targeted individuals could be subject to up to sixteen hours' detention at home a day and even internal exile away from family. Although control orders were replaced in 2011 by terrorism protection and investigation measures (TPIMs) following further judicial criticism,[30] they are similar measures to control orders. They remain draconian, allowing a range of measures to be imposed covering all aspects of a targeted individual's life: residence, travel, movement, financial services, property, electronic communications devices, association, work, and study, and are backed by reporting, polygraphy, drug testing, photography, monitoring, appointments, and residency information. Legal challenges to control orders and TPIMs are subject to special procedures including the holding of hearings in private, the with-holding of evidence and reasons, and the appointment of a special advocate to represent the person subject to the control order. Again, we see the exceptional nature of the counter-terrorism legal regime. Normally we would expect to see trials held in public, and that the accused should be able to see all the evidence against them and choose legal counsel.

While terrorism seems ever present in our lives, the number of individuals subject to TPIMs is small, and the risk of terrorism for the ordinary citizen is low. In contrast, the state's surveillance powers impact a signifi-cant part of the population, including many who are not aware of such activities and are not engaged in criminal behaviour. The Regulation of Investigatory Powers Act (RIPA) 2000 covers different forms of surveillance by the police and other law enforcement agencies, includ-ing the security and intelligence services. These activi-ties can be authorised by designated persons within law enforcement organisations on national security grounds as well as to detect crimes.

RIPA also brings the conduct and use of covert human intelligence sources (CHIS) – informants and under-cover police officers – within a statutory framework. Remarkably, since 2021 criminal conduct by CHIS has been permitted in the interests of national security, for the purpose of preventing or detecting crime, preventing disorder, or in the interests of the economic well-being of the UK,[31] in effect giving a CHIS 'statutory impunity'.[32] Further, the Court of Appeal held that a policy that authorised MI5 officers to run undercover agents who participated in the commission of criminal offences was lawful.[33] We see another example of state agents or those working for the state being placed outside the criminal law when they are acting in pursuit of national security.

A person who alleges that they are subject to improper surveillance may make a complaint to the Investigatory Powers Tribunal (IPT), though most individuals subject to surveillance will, by its covert nature, be unaware that they are being targeted. The interception of communications is now governed by the Investigatory Powers Act 2016, described as a 'formidable statute', whose 'highly technical and complex provisions ... mask extraordinary powers of surveillance'.[34] This is especially so in the power given to the home secretary to grant both targeted warrants and warrants for the interception and acquisition of bulk data at the request of one of the heads of the intelligence services.

Challenges to bulk data warrants have been dismissed by the courts. In the *Liberty* case, the High Court declared that the government had 'far greater experience of dealing with' matters of national security 'than a court could possibly have'. The court also pointed to the 'democratic legitimacy' of the home secretary who was 'accountable to Parliament'.[35] The home secretary's decisions to grant certain warrants must, since the 2016 Act, be approved by a judicial commissioner, who is tasked with applying the same principles of review as a court, potentially representing a significant judicial limitation on executive powers. However, the evidence is that while the government stresses judicial oversight when persuading Parliament to adopt new national security legislation, it is very critical of judges fulfilling their statutory functions once the law is in force.[36]

The National Security Act 2023 reflects a concern that terrorism is not the only current threat to the UK. The Act returns to state threats which, apart from Northern Ireland, dominated UK security policies during the Cold War. The National Security Act 2023 modernises a number of espionage offences found in various Official Secrets Acts with the aim of making it harder for other states to conduct hostile acts targeted at the UK. These acts include espionage, interference in the UK's political system, sabotage, and assassination. Fear of terrorism is now matched by fear of foreign agents.

Judicial checks on power

I have already mentioned a number of important cases, and readers will have gained an impression of the courts' deferential attitude towards government action when that action is declared to be in the defence of the realm or in pursuit of national security. Those are matters primarily or sometimes exclusively for the government. When the Campaign for Nuclear Disarmament (CND) sought to challenge the government's decision to go to war against Iraq in 2003 on the basis that it was illegal under international law, the Court dismissed it in no uncertain terms, declaring that 'domestic courts do not rule on questions of international law which affect foreign sovereign states'.[37]

Governments and judges are generally in agreement that 'judicial deference to the executive on national security matters is necessary due to judges' lack of democratic accountability'.[38] However, the resulting lack of balance of power seems to have allowed the government to take coercive and, on occasions, brutal measures within the UK and previously in its colonies with little opportunity for real accountability before the courts. It is unsurprising to find that the government has also been reluctant to recognise and remedy wrongs committed by its agents. The government may pay compensation following adverse judgments but, in other instances, very little is forthcoming; even apologies are grudgingly given.

Following initial recognition by the courts of legal claims brought by some of the victims of the Kenyan concentration camps of the 1950s, in 2013 the government announced a settlement for over 5,000 individuals amounting to nearly £20 million. Other 'legacy' cases arising out of abuses by colonial authorities have not been remedied, particularly when blocked by the courts. Such was the case that arose out of the alleged murder of twenty-four civilians by Scots Guards in the village of Batang Kali in Malaya in 1948.[39] Closer to home, it was only after a second public inquiry into the events of

Bloody Sunday found in 2010 that the killing of fourteen unarmed protestors by British paratroopers in Derry in 1972 was unjustified,[40] that the government offered compensation to the families of the victims. Bearing in mind that a constitution is supposed to regulate the relationship between the state and individuals under its authority, the legal framework in the UK seems to weigh heavily in favour of the state and fails to protect even the most basic rights of individuals when it is deemed that the state has been acting in defence of the realm or in pursuit of national security.

Human rights law has made some inroads into government impunity for the actions of its armed forces and security services, but it has not triggered successful challenges to the source of the power to deploy the armed forces or utilise the security services. The claimants in the *Gentle* case of 2008 were the mothers of two nineteen-year-old soldiers who lost their lives in Iraq. Their claim was that the government's failure to obtain reliable legal advice led to a decision to go to war in 2003 which, if proper advice had been taken, would not have been made and consequently the soldiers' lives would not have been lost. To win this argument would require the courts to decide on the legality of the decision to go to war. The judges were simply not willing to do this. According to Lady Hale it was beyond the competence of the courts to rule on the legality of the use of force against Iraq, so it was not possible to read into the ECHR a duty not to send soldiers to an illegal war.[41]

Remarkably, despite all we have seen about courts' reluctance to challenge government on these issues, there has recently been a pushback against so-called 'judicial imperialism', which argues that judges are increasingly expanding their understanding of the protections provided under the ECHR. It is claimed that this has led to a 'fog of law', inhibiting the armed forces from achieving their objectives. The picture painted is that of military commanders always looking over their shoulder in case a claim is made against them, or laboriously halting operations to seek legal advice.[42] Such criticisms of the judiciary have been put in no uncertain terms: '[n]one have succeeded in defeating the armed forces of the United Kingdom. Napoleon, Falkenhayn and Hitler could not. But where these enemies failed, our own legal institutions threaten to succeed'.[43] This was not written by a politician but by a judge of the Court of Appeal. Nonetheless, it remains an exercise in hyperbole.

The main court judgment that provoked such an outcry was *Smith v MoD*, delivered by the Supreme Court in 2013.[44] The case involved a claim brought by the mother of a soldier killed in Iraq in an under-protected Snatch Land Rover (in the dark humour of the military these vehicles were known as 'mobile coffins'). The claimants succeeded in gaining recognition from the Court that the ECHR protected individuals within the UK but also applied in other countries when the UK exercised forms of control. This meant that civilians under UK control should benefit from human rights protections, as established in 2011 by the ECtHR in the *Al-Skeini* case where Iraqi civilians in British-occupied Basra had been shot by British soldiers.[45] The importance of *Smith v MoD*, however, was to make it clear that British soldiers themselves should benefit particularly from the right to life under Article 2 of the ECHR. Soldiers are duty bound to follow orders and so are clearly within the control of the UK wherever they may be, and therefore the Court felt should indeed benefit from the protections provided by the ECHR.

This did not mean, however, that the right to life had been automatically violated in the *Smith v MoD* case. It was only violated if it could be proven that the MoD had not taken adequate measures to ensure that the troops deployed to Iraq were properly equipped, not necessarily with the best equipment, but with equipment that was more than adequate for the job at hand. Although this issue was not litigated before the courts, the government did eventually accept liability in 2017. However, this was only following criticism in the Iraq Inquiry Report of the inadequacies of Snatch Land Rovers, particularly when used to confront a violent insurgency where IEDs were a routine form of attack on British forces.[46]

Snatch Land Rovers themselves were initially used in Northern Ireland by the British Army to move rapidly into a hostile area to grab suspected terrorists, who were then detained without trial or, where there was sufficient evidence, subject to trial without a jury before so-called Diplock Courts. Snatching someone on the streets of

Belfast or Basra and interning them in detention centres run by the British Army would seem to embody the type of control that engages the protections of the ECHR. However, the courts, through labyrinthine reasoning, have ruled the power to detain in Iraq and Afghanistan was regulated by the law of armed conflict, which does not provide for a full range of legal protections under human rights law.[47]

However, this was not the case in Northern Ireland. There, the government had refused to accept that there was an armed conflict between itself and the IRA during the Troubles, and so its policy of detention was consequently subject to the ECHR.[48] The advantage for the armed forces in applying the laws of armed conflict to detention is that they do not require the review of ongoing detentions by a court, as is needed under Article 5 of the ECHR.

The treatment of individuals while in detention should be, and clearly is, within the remit of human rights law, whatever the context. The death of Baha Mousa, a hotel worker detained by British forces in Basra, who was beaten to death by British soldiers, seems to have gained maximum coverage in term of accountability. This killing led to a finding of violation of the right to life by the UK in an ECtHR judgment.[49] In addition, British soldiers involved in the abuse were prosecuted before a court martial and one, Corporal Payne, was convicted of the war crime of inhuman treatment (though he was cleared of manslaughter). Payne became the first and only British soldier convicted of a war crime under the International Criminal Court Act 2001. However, the Baha Mousa Inquiry led by Sir William Gage demonstrated that responsibility for Baha Mousa's death should have extended to those higher up the chain of command.[50] Overall, the government was held to account under the ECHR, a soldier under British military law, and the MoD and military by a public inquiry. Justice may have seen to be done by such extensive scrutiny, but only Payne served time – a derisory twelve months.

The evidence from investigations by the International Criminal Court (ICC) is that abuse by a minority of British soldiers in Iraq was much more widespread than has been uncovered by any of these UK-led processes.[51] In making out-of-court payments of over £20 million to nearly over 1,500 claims from Iraqi nationals, the government has recognised its broader culpability at least by its actions, though the MoD has stated that 'the reason for the settlement of the overwhelming majority of claims is not ... that the MoD accepts that the claimants were maltreated', rather they were wrongly imprisoned.[52]

In Afghanistan there have been allegations of special forces' death squads which are subject to a review,[53] and the conviction in 2013 of a sergeant in the Royal Marines (Alexander Blackman, referred to initially as 'Marine A') for the unlawful killing of a severely wounded Taliban insurgent. The court martial convicted him of the crime of murder, which was eventually reduced to manslaughter on the grounds of diminished responsibility on a second appeal following a public outcry whipped up by certain politicians, the media, and the author Frederick Forsythe.[54] The limited chances of detecting and prosecuting war crimes in a combat zone like Afghanistan are demonstrated by the fact that it was only because Blackman's act was captured on an illicit headcam worn by another soldier that prosecution was pursued. One unadopted proposal coming out of this appalling incident was that soldiers should be required to wear headcams.[55] The practical application of the rule of law to the military when on operations is an ongoing problem and leads to double standards. The government is fond of pointing to the justice of its military expeditions against various forms of evil or criminal enemies, but is unhappy if its soldiers are exposed to prosecution for war crimes.

The gradual encroachment of human rights jurisprudence into cases arising from the Troubles in Northern Ireland effectively shifted the judicial spotlight onto the government and its use of armed soldiers in a situation of extreme violence. In the *McCann* case,[56] the British authorities were aware of a planned IRA attack in Gibraltar, involving the detonation of a car bomb. Special Air Services (SAS) soldiers shot dead three IRA suspects in the belief that they were about to detonate the bomb. The ECtHR decided that the killings by the soldiers did not a violate the right to life under Article 2 of the ECHR, 'but there was a violation of the right to life by the United Kingdom because sufficient precautions had not been taken to avoid the death of the suspects'.[57]

The ruling questioned the UK's decision to use the military in place of police forces in times of peace, especially as these were special forces from the SAS Regiment.[58]

The ECtHR has, though, been inconsistent in requiring the government to take measures to reduce the risk of loss of life when undertaking armed military or police operations. The lack of due diligence by the police did not appear to be viewed as relevant by the Court in the case of Jean Charles de Menezes.[59] Specialist firearms officers shot dead de Menezes in the mistaken belief he was a suicide bomber, in the febrile atmosphere following the 7 July 2005 (7/7) attacks, which had killed over fifty people in London. The protection provided by due diligence duties is thus limited, tending to kick in, if at all, after the event as an exercise in lessons to be learned.

This can be seen more recently in litigation arising out of the Manchester Arena terrorist bombing of 2017. The claims also showed that giving the security services a statutory basis has not necessarily improved the position of the citizen in relation to the state. A public inquiry, led by Sir John Saunders, had unearthed evidence to suggest that MI5 had not taken appropriate measures to prevent the terror attack on the Manchester Arena, in particular that it had failed to assess evidence against the suicide bomber (Salman Abedi) as terror related.[60] The claim by the families of victims was brought before the Investigatory Powers Tribunal. The claim under Articles 2 (right to life) and 3 (freedom from inhuman or degrading treatment) of the ECHR was dismissed by the

Tribunal as being out of time, despite the fact that it was only in 2023 that the potential failure of MI5 had been unearthed by the inquiry. The Tribunal stated that even if the claim had been brought in time, though, it would have led to MI5 using up valuable time and resources in defending the claim.

MI5 could, of course, have chosen not to defend the claim and admit that it could have done better to protect the lives of innocent concert goers. The claimants had to be satisfied with a guarded apology by the director of MI5 instead. It seems that the needs of 'national' security, perversely including the valuable time of MI5, outweighed the security of the individual, despite the failure by the state to take adequate measures to protect crowded spaces from terrorist or similar attacks.[61]

This brief, and inevitably incomplete review, shows that over time the courts have been empowered by the ECHR and have made advances in protecting the rights of citizens (including in limited cases the citizens of other countries) and British soldiers. However, these judgments have been at most a hindrance and annoyance to the government; they have not taken away the government's power to deploy forces potentially in breach of international laws prohibiting the use of force. It is no surprise that the massive kinetic force used by the armed forces has led to claims against the government for violations of the human rights of victims. And again, it should be no surprise to the government that some of these claims have succeeded. Equally, it should not come as a shock that British soldiers can commit war crimes – whether it's the killing of a wounded combatant, or the beating to death of a defenceless detainee. The fact that very few soldiers have been convicted should not be taken as evidence that these are the only war crimes which have been committed by British forces in Iraq and Afghanistan.

3

The Political Constitution

Emergency and war powers

As we have seen in the last chapter, although lacking an overarching constitutional framework, there is a broad patchwork of laws covering defence. This leaves much to be dealt with in the 'political constitution' where government, and more broadly executive decision-making powers, dominate. War powers are subject to non-binding constitutional conventions. They are broad and potentially devastating, ranging from defending the UK (and historically the Empire) from external attacks and threats, military intervention, and, ultimately, regime change.

As well as war powers exercised in the face of external threats, the government has a range of emergency powers connected to national security within the UK, including preventing and responding to terrorism and various forms of internal unrest. Although some of these powers have been put on a statutory basis (e.g. Terrorism Act 2000, Civil Contingencies Act 2004, Investigatory Powers Act 2016, and National Security Act 2023), discretionary powers, whether found within statutes or in the unwritten prerogative, remain dominant. Although the legal constitution may appear to be expanding at the expense of the political, as shown by the adoption of increasing amounts of security legislation, this does not by itself increase regulation of discretionary powers. Indeed, it can lead to an increase in executive power and a significant reduction in the rights and liberties of individuals.

Civilian control of the military

One of the fundamental principles underpinning the political constitution is that the armed forces remain under the control of the civilian authorities, in both peacetime and wartime. The source of this principle is found in the English Civil Wars of 1642–9. They involved a constitutional struggle fought over sovereign power remaining in the hands of the King or becoming embodied in the supremacy of Parliament.[1] The victory of the Parliamentarians through the military successes of Cromwell's New Model Army created enormous tension between a powerful and increasingly unconstrained military and the civil authority of Parliament. General Monck, who was instrumental in the restoration of the monarchy, declared that the 'army in England has broken up the Parliament, out of a restless ambition to govern themselves ... For my part, I think myself obliged, by the duty of my place, to keep the military power in obedience to the civil'.

The Civil War was a conflict between the monarch

and Parliament but, with the restoration of the monarchy, prerogative powers over the military were once again in the hands of the monarch, and it was only through the gradual transference of prerogative powers from the monarch to the government that we truly saw civilian control over the military. But, this was the power of government rather than that of Parliament. True, the Bill of Rights 1689 asserted that the continued existence of the armed forces required the regular approval of Parliament, but operational control of the armed forces involving crucial decisions to deploy forces within the UK and overseas was firmly in the hands of the government.

Civil–military relations should be central to the legal constitution and yet, while Parliament asserted ultimate authority over the army in the Bill of Rights, the military was, and to an extent remains, a separate society governed by separate rules.[2] This partly explains the ambiguity that exists in the position of the military within society and its position within the political constitution rather than the legal. Although the Armed Forces Act 2006 details the military and criminal offences applicable to service personnel, it does not specify or delimit the powers of the military. In contrast, the police and the security services' activities are governed by legislation – the Police and Criminal Evidence Act 1984 and the Security Services Act 1989 – bringing them more clearly within the legal constitution.

Despite the lack of clarity about the legal powers of

the military, the unwritten principle of civilian control and the absence historically of military rule in the UK has created the strong belief that the military is under the effective control of the government. A military takeover might seem to be something from the realms of fiction. The political and military establishment maintains the view that the military should remain neutral in political affairs. However, this did not stop rumours of a possible military takeover during the turbulent years of the Labour government of Harold Wilson in the 1970s, or mutterings of mutiny in the face of the possibility of a disarming Corbyn-led Labour government in 2015.

Although the ghost of martial law (military rule) seems to have been laid to rest centuries ago, with Dicey declaring that it 'is unknown to the law of England',[3] it remains possible that the military could flex its muscles were the state threatened from within or from an outside threat, or were the military's own existence to come under threat. If that materialises then a form of martial law might follow, dug up, no doubt, from the dusty vaults of constitutional history.[4]

Martial law is a spectral presence in British history, described by the Duke of Wellington as 'neither more nor less than the will of the general who commands the army; in fact, martial law means no law at all'. The general declaring martial law and directing his soldiers to carry it out 'is bound to lay down the rules, regulations and limits, according to which his will is to be carried out'. Wellington was cited in a case of 1867, where there was extensive but inconclusive discussion of the source, meaning, and practice of martial law. While it was said to be a prerogative power declared by governors in some colonies when the authorities were faced with rebellions, and by generals in cases of military occupations overseas, it was said not to have been used in England. However, it was agreed that if it were, a proclamation of martial law would amount to giving authority to the military 'to do whatever they think expedient for the public safety'.[5]

In British colonies, the government, operating through the governor of the colony, gave military and security forces extensive 'emergency' powers to address unrest. This came to a head in the brutal violence that erupted towards the end of empire. In response to the Mau Mau uprising in Kenya in the 1950s, the British authorities responded by instituting a state of emergency, empowering the army and security services to respond with 'massive coercion'. Military measures included prohibited zones where effectively a shoot-to-kill policy operated, protected villages involving the forced displacement of many civilians, extensive bombing of areas where insurgents and civilians were present, Emergency Assize Courts presiding over multiple hangings, and detention without trial in concentration camps 'where people were dehumanized and randomly brutalized (or just murdered)'.[6] The veneer of civilian control could not mask unregulated and extensive state violence.

Along with the US, the UK was an occupying power in Iraq in 2003–4 after ousting the regime of Saddam

Hussein. The military exercised powers of arrest, detention, and the use of force to tackle the growing insurgency. It was empowered to do this under the Fourth Geneva Convention 1949. However, Iraq reveals the problem of a relatively small military power trying to control a vast and violent territory. In the early part of the occupation of southern Iraq, a senior British officer boasted that the British Army was the 'biggest and best gang in Basra'.[7] It soon ceased to be able to make that claim as the insurgency grew in intensity and British forces were stretched beyond their limits. In that desperate situation, in some instances, abuses were committed against suspected insurgents and civilians. Although not martial law in the sense discussed above, there was a sense of soldiers taking the law into their own hands.

Citizens in uniform? The military and national emergencies

Civil authorities, the police, and the security services all have responsibility to maintain law and order and protect the security of citizens and other individuals within the state. The military remains largely in the background but there are times when its presence is felt. The police are often inanely viewed as 'citizens in uniform' who police by consent, though they have the power of arrest and have authority to use force. These are referred to as 'police', 'law enforcement', or sometimes 'constabulary' powers.[8] Leading constitutional lawyers have described the depiction of the police as 'citizens in uniform' as a 'comical trope', pointing to the extensive powers exclusively given to the modern police under the Police and Criminal Evidence Act 1984: principally of stop and search, arrest, detention, questioning, and entry search and seizure.[9]

The phrase 'citizens in uniform' has also been applied to the military.[10] However, this is largely in the context of the debate about whether soldiers have the same rights as citizens or whether they have given up some or all of those rights when becoming soldiers.[11] Considering a soldier's duty to obey orders, which regularly involves putting their lives at risk, their rights certainly seem to be more limited than the civilian–citizen.

The phrase 'citizen in uniform' has also been used in explaining the role of the military in facing rioters. The Riot Act of 1714 was extensively used by local authorities to break up illegally assembled groups of twelve or more. In practice, the military could be called in aid of such actions, sometimes leading to atrocities such as the 'Peterloo Massacre' in Manchester of 1819, where mounted soldiers charged a large, peaceful yet illegally assembled crowd, which had been demanding greater representation in Parliament, causing some deaths and many injuries. While the speakers were convicted of sedition, the soldiers were exonerated. Nevertheless, the Peterloo Massacre 'demonstrated the unsuitability of military personnel for policing crowds and demonstrations'.[12]

When facing riots the precarious legal position of the

armed forces becomes apparent, with military personnel most commonly being likened to citizens rather than soldiers – most famously by Lord Mansfield in 1781 in a case arising out of the Gordon Riots when nearly 300 rioters were killed by troops. This legal fiction, meaning that soldiers have no more rights in such situations than civilians, was shown to be inadequate in justifying the actions of soldiers during the Troubles in Northern Ireland, which stretched from their initial deployment in 1969 until the Good Friday Peace Agreement of 1998.

Lord Diplock stated that in these circumstances to describe a soldier as 'an ordinary citizen in uniform' was 'misleading'. This was said in a case arising from the shooting dead of an unarmed individual who had run away from an army patrol after being told to halt. The soldier's actions clearly went beyond the right of an ordinary citizen to self-defence but were not condemned by the court. This seemed to be due to the circumstances in which the army was 'employed in aid of the civil power in Northern Ireland', where it was faced with 'an armed and clandestinely organised insurrection against the lawful government of Her Majesty by persons seeking to gain political ends by violent means'. Unlike a citizen in such a situation, a soldier 'is under a duty, enforceable under military law, ... to risk his own life should this be necessary in preventing terrorist acts', and 'in the performance of this duty he is armed with ... a self-loading rifle, from which a bullet ... is almost certain to cause serious injury if not death'.[13]

The legal basis of the use of state-sanctioned armed and potentially deadly force in Northern Ireland has remained unclear. We do know that soldiers were subject to peacetime criminal laws rather than those international laws governing armed conflicts, since the government of the UK steadfastly refused to recognise the Troubles as an armed conflict (though the IRA claimed that it was). But the criminal law seemed to have limited traction on the actions of soldiers. Having said that, there *were* some prosecutions of soldiers, notoriously that of Private Clegg, who shot dead a back-seat passenger in a car driven by a joyrider as it drove through a checkpoint he was manning. He was initially convicted of murder which was eventually overturned.[14]

A significant number of legacy cases arising from the Troubles remain outstanding, though there have been attempts to prevent these coming before the courts.[15] Significantly, we see the encroachment into this uncertain constitutional landscape of human rights law as cases against the UK were brought, with mixed success, by some of the victims' families, alleging violations of the right to life.[16] Overall, there are many examples of transgressions by the military and only a limited number of successful prosecutions of soldiers and human rights challenges against the government for the acts of its soldiers. The failure to hold soldiers and the government to account for massacres such as occurred on Bloody Sunday 1972 indicates that although we can identify aspects of the legal constitution governing the military, we are at the thin end of legality, where lethal force is sanctioned, and the unlawful use of deadly force often goes unpunished.

In contrast to the armed forces, the history of organised police forces in the UK begins later. These were established first in London and the counties under the Metropolitan Police Act 1829 and the County and Borough Police Act 1856. Despite the enhanced police function in the UK, the military continues to be called upon by civil authorities. Although the Riot Act was read for the last time by civil authorities in 1919 in the face of unrest in Liverpool, where again the military was extensively used, troops have been deployed many times since in support of civil authorities under prerogative powers. In recent years, troops were deployed in response to security threats to Heathrow in 2003, to provide security for the London Olympics in 2012, and following a terrorist attack in Manchester in 2017. Plans were put in place in 2019 to deploy troops in the face of unrest following Brexit.

These deployments have occurred despite the constitutional unease that surrounds the use of the armed forces within the UK during peacetime, which can be traced back to the reaction to Charles I's extensive use of such powers in the lead-up to outbreak of civil war in 1642. However, it is true to say that the convention seems to be that the military should only act in aid of the civil authorities at their request and in limited circumstances and that, in a mature democracy, threats to security should be dealt with by civilian authorities.

Constitutionally speaking, the legal basis of the power to deploy troops to confront internal disturbances is said to derive either from the legal constitution – the Emergency Powers Acts 1920 and 1964 and the Civil Contingencies Act 2004 – or the political, in the form of prerogative powers which can be instigated without any formal declaration of a state of emergency.[17] Although described as residual, in practice internal troop deployments are normally made under prerogative powers. Michael Head also notes that the Ministry of Defence itself has identified two further legal bases for troop deployment. First, a 'common-law tenet' derived from judicial statements, which demonstrates that 'members of the armed forces have a duty to provide the support normally expected of the ordinary citizen'. Secondly, 'Queen's Regulations place an additional duty on military commanders to act on their own responsibility without a request by a civil agency where in exceptional circumstances, a grave and sudden emergency has arisen, which in the opinion of the Commander demands his immediate intervention to protect life or property'.[18] Rather worryingly this appears to give military commanders discretion to deploy without first gaining civilian approval.

In addition, the government has codified emergency powers to tackle specific threats such as terrorism and more recently the coronavirus pandemic,[19] but the power to deploy troops has its basis in the sources identified in this section, with the default position being the use of prerogative powers. As summarised by Head and Mann: '[t]aken as a whole, considerable legal powers are said to exist to authorise calling out the troops to deal with a wide variety of alleged threats to society, including civil unrest, industrial action and acts of terrorism, and these measures have been augmented by the "almost boundless power" that can be asserted under' the Civil Contingencies Act 2004.[20]

War powers

In the UK, the decision to go to war or otherwise commit UK armed forces or assets to foreign lands remains a prerogative power, originally belonging to the Crown but now in the hands of the prime minister acting within the Cabinet, or a small part of it known as the war cabinet. Given that prerogative powers bypass normal methods of democratic control, and can be exercised without parliamentary approval, there is pressure in the modern era to re-evaluate the balance between recognising the need for efficient decision-making and the demands of democratic accountability.

In general terms, prerogative war powers have two serious consequences for both the rule of law and democratic accountability. First of all, there is no legal requirement to secure parliamentary approval before action is taken under prerogative war powers. Legally, the decision to go to war or otherwise commit UK armed forces or assets to foreign lands remains a prerogative power and thus can be exercised without parliamentary approval. Politically, there is the question, since the Iraq war of 2003, of whether there is a non-legally binding convention creating an expectation that the government seek prior parliamentary approval for a deployment of forces overseas. The second consequence is that the courts do not encroach on the competence of the executive by asserting a power to review the decisions of the Crown on the disposition and use of the UK's armed forces.[21] This is despite a gradual judicial encroachment into other aspects of prerogative powers.[22]

Judicial abstinence on reviewing the government's exercise of war powers has meant that successive governments 'have endorsed [an] increasingly expansive, and seemingly self-serving, interpretation of several international legal frameworks governing the use of force' without any legal check.[23] The unwillingness of the courts to apply international laws to decisions to go to war, together with the absence of any substantive national legal principles, result in the complete absence of judicial review by British courts of any such decisions. More broadly, the courts perceive international relations and national security as beyond their purview, viewing them as matters for the government exercising its political judgement.[24]

War powers decision-making based on a largely unaccountable exercise of prerogative powers seems to be an anachronism, a vestige of the monarch as the commander-in-chief of the armed forces. Democratic control over the exercise of war powers is stronger in most other European countries than in the UK.[25] The case for increasing democratic accountability to balance executive and military efficiency is now overwhelming but seems to be increasingly difficult to achieve. Before 2003, it was true to say that 'precedents exist for permitting MPs a substantive prior vote before taking military action; but a greater number of precedents exist for MPs being sidelined'.[26]

After 2003, we have to consider whether the government's war powers have been restricted by a non-binding convention which began to emerge in the lead-up to the invasion of Iraq in 2003, ultimately leading to a debate in the Commons and a vote on the invasion.[27] This should have been a turning point in democratic accountability, especially given the gamut of unintended and disastrous consequences that flowed from the decision to go to war. However, the existence, let alone the exact nature, of this convention remains unclear, as the debates over Libya in 2011 and Syria in 2013 and 2018 show.

In 2011 the RAF was deployed to enforce a no-fly zone and to defend civilians in the face of an imminent attack on Benghazi by the forces of Colonel Gaddafi. A debate and a vote in Parliament was held only after initial deployment. This was justified by the need for rapid military action in the face of an existential threat to Libyan civilians. Some months later, the Cabinet Manual of 2011 was published, which states that the government acknowledged a convention had 'developed in Parliament that before troops were committed the House of Commons should have an opportunity to debate the matter ... except when there was an emergency and such action would not be appropriate'.[28]

In deciding whether to respond to chemical weapons attacks on civilians in Syria by the Assad regime in 2013, the government's proposal to launch airstrikes was put before the House of Commons and voted down, meaning that the government led by Prime Minister Cameron did not proceed with the airstrikes. Prior parliamentary approval was sought and gained by Prime Minister Cameron to use force against the Islamic State in Iraq in 2014, and then for the extension of the operation to Syria in 2015.

In contrast to the Cameron years, where respect for the convention reached its highpoint, Prime Minister Theresa May launched airstrikes on Syria in April 2018 in response to the further use of chemical weapons by the Assad regime without first seeking parliamentary approval, even though it was not made clear that this was an 'emergency' within the meaning of the convention.[29]

Fast-forward to the present, and debate in the House of Commons was held after the airstrikes on the Houthis in Yemen in January 2024, taken in response to their attacks on shipping in the Red Sea.[30] The government made it clear that there were 'no plans for a retrospective vote' in the House of Commons 'as parliamentary approval' was 'not required for military action'.[31]

In explaining this to the House of Commons a few days after the airstrikes, the prime minister stated that 'the need to maximise the security and effectiveness of the operation meant that it was not possible to bring this matter to the House in advance'.[32] Prime Minister Sunak further stated that this was 'in accordance with the convention. I remain committed to that convention, and would always look to follow appropriate processes and procedures, and act in line with precedent ... there were strikes in 2015 and 2018, when a similar process was followed'.[33] The leader of the opposition seemed to agree with the government, noting that the military action against the Houthis was different to the deployment of troops when Parliament must be informed beforehand.[34] In these exchanges, the convention seems to be a reference point but it does not seem to bind the government.

Changing understandings of the convention by the government when making decisions to deploy troops or armed forces have eroded any real improvements in democratic accountability following the vote on Iraq in 2003. The terms of the convention are very general given that it does not require a prior vote in Parliament (only an opportunity to debate the matter). It also uses a much-abused term – 'emergency' – to define the exception.

There was no discernible discussion of the convention or any need for parliamentary debate when the government decided to deploy air and sea forces to help defend Israel from Iranian missile and drone strikes in October 2024. The democratic deficit is extraordinary given that such decisions could easily drag the UK into a wider war in the Middle East.

In general, the debate over the existence and scope of a post-2003 convention revolves around highly visible uses of force. In contrast to clear uses of kinetic force, a hidden problem is that, with the development of both hybrid and remote warfare, much military and defence activity may not be visible, or else deemed insufficient to trigger parliamentary questions or debate. Hybrid warfare has been characterised as 'an operational approach to warfighting that uses an explicit mix of military and non-military tactics'.[35] Remote warfare is 'characterised by the use of drones, special forces, private military companies (PMCs), and so on'.[36] Together, 'these are modes of ... warfare that avoid large-scale, highly visible, traditional military operations involving ground troops'.[37] It has been pointed out that there is a 'growing preference for warfare by remote control, such as the deployment of drones or military trainers', or the use of private contractors, which are 'perceived as' forms 'of intervention with less skin in the game'. One consequence being that such actions have been taken increasingly 'without Parliamentary approval – and without scrutiny'.[38]

There may be other forms of accountability for drone strikes and other 'remote' forms of force, though. There was, for example, a Joint Committee report into drone usage after the targeted killing of Reyaad Khan, a UK citizen, in Syria in 2015.[39] However, the prior or even subsequent approval of Parliament is not deemed necessary for any such strike. It seems to be accepted practice that targeted killings by drone strikes and by special forces escape political scrutiny. After reviewing this practice, Matt Bennett concludes with justification that it must be 'a matter of fundamental constitutional concern that there exists in the UK a source of executive political power that ... is used to authorise the targeted killing of suspected terrorists ... without either legal or political oversight of ... any meaningful sort on the domestic plane'.[40] Furthermore, the lack of political accountability is disguised by the government using the cloak of international law, no matter how inaccurate the legal argument is, to effectively claim that the proposed actions are 'constitutional' by dint of their alleged compliance with international law.[41] This is not only the case with targeted killings but also with other overseas military operations, as we shall see in Chapter 4.

It appears that the convention can readily be pushed aside when the government of the day, for whatever political reason, does not want to risk a debate and a possible negative vote in Parliament. Political pressure to hold debates and votes prior to major troop deployments to combat zones may be too great for the government to resist but, apart from that, the convention seems to have been hollowed out. In assessing the role of parliamentary scrutiny and approval in the light of developments in modern warfare, and in particular the UK's increasing practice of remote warfare, it has been argued that a consistent and legitimate way to increase effective accountability will be to identify and clarify the avenues for democratic scrutiny, and to clarify their use in a more formal but non-binding War Powers Resolution or a legally binding War Powers Act. In particular, that instrument should specify when Parliament should be engaged before force is used and when it should be involved afterwards.[42]

Parliamentary approval for the deployment of armed forces

War powers decision-making based on the largely unaccountable exercise of prerogative powers seems to be an anachronism, a vestige of the monarch as the commander-in-chief of the armed forces. Medieval monarchs were the embodiment of a nation's sovereignty and power, but they often struggled to raise armies, relying heavily on mercenaries and having to raise funds for each military campaign. In some ways the modern British government is much more powerful and efficient, having at its disposal well-resourced and professional armed forces, which are deployable around the world at limited notice. Put in such stark terms, the case for increasing democratic accountability to balance increased executive and military efficiency seems overwhelming.

A clearer war powers convention or a stronger war powers statute requiring a debate and a substantive vote in Parliament before deployment of British troops in an armed conflict would improve accountability. This would not only hold the executive accountable, but the process itself would promote the 'efficient and effective performance of the required task' since it would make the government 'gather information and ... exchange ideas with those calling [it] to account'.[43] In other words, the government must convince Parliament that deploying military forces is the correct approach to a crisis situation.

Going to war is an action undertaken on behalf of the whole country, and Parliament uniquely represents that constituency. However, Parliament has to be properly informed. The prime minister usually outlines the political, military, security, and humanitarian reasons for any action, as well as its international legal basis. Regrettably, the latter is usually based on a sanitised version of the attorney general's advice, the redaction of which is justified by a constitutional convention against making public the full legal advice.[44] As I argue in Chapter 4, Parliament needs to be properly briefed if it is to make decisions about the deployment of forces, and the full legal advice given to the government should accordingly be released. MPs will then have to make up their minds based on a balance of legal, humanitarian, and military considerations.

War powers have been clearly located throughout history within the political constitution. Politicians are elected and chosen to make these decisions, meaning that the courts have generally refused to intercede based on an understanding of the constitution in which defence and national security are within the political realm. However, this does not mean that on the political side war powers belong exclusively to the government. Indeed, it is the ultimate responsibility of Parliament to ensure that the might of the UK state is used lawfully and legitimately.

I have argued that parliamentary approval for the use of armed forces overseas should be a clear constitutional rule. The regulation of the prerogative to deploy troops is almost exclusively discussed in terms of war powers and the deployment of armed forces overseas. However, we must not forget the admonition of General Monck in the seventeenth century that Parliament should exercise control of the actions of the military within the state as well. This would mean that significant troop deployments within the UK ordered by the executive to address emergencies should also be debated and approved by Parliament. In simple terms, the exercise of military might, at home or abroad, should be openly debated and approved by Parliament unless the country is under attack and there is no time to convene Parliament, or in the case of emergencies at home, when it is necessary to act first and debate later – for example in trying to prevent major flooding or a terrorist attack. Only within these narrow confines of self-defence and necessity can democratic accountability justifiably be pushed back to after the event.

Political accountability
As might be expected in the field of defence, which remains dominated by the political constitution,

accountability is primarily down to Parliament and select committees of MPs. This might appear to be politicians marking their own homework but, sometimes at least, the members of the relevant select committee can operate independently from government and party.

In this way, Parliament should exercise scrutiny over government decision-making, not only on war powers and national emergencies, but on other key aspects of defence and security. Unfortunately, there is often insufficient scrutiny of the executive due to the government's control of the majority in Parliament. A good example of the lack of real parliamentary oversight is in the setting of the defence budget, which remains a political football with politicians falling over themselves to promise increased defence spending in the Trump era. In February 2025, against the backdrop of President Trump's clear disdain towards NATO, Prime Minister Sir Keir Starmer announced the biggest sustained increase in defence spending since the end of the cold war. The headline figure given was 2.5 per cent of GDP from 2027, though this was increased to 2.6 per cent by the prime minister in updating the definition of defence to include the contribution of the intelligence and security services. The need to defend the country in the face of growing threats from Russia and China, and the desire to placate an increasingly unstable ally, were given political preference to development aid, which was cut from 0.5 per cent to 0.3 per cent of GDP to pay for the increased defence spend. It is worth noting that the UN's target for development aid is 0.7 per cent. The UK's values can be dramatically changed by a political decision of the government with little constitutional restraint.

However, the veneer of constitutionality is maintained by the constitutional principle, established by the Bill of Rights of 1689, that the raising of money for the Crown's use without the approval of Parliament is illegal. In modern terms, Parliament must authorise the government's proposed expenditure and the raising of taxation to finance it. Although this appears to give Parliament the 'power of the purse' there is little scrutiny of proposed budgets by Parliament, with the government using its majority in the Commons to gain the necessary support. Obtaining the assent of the House of Lords to the budget is a formality. Beyond this, defence spending from the regular budget can be supplemented to meet unforeseen expenditure, such as unanticipated military operations, by funds drawn from the Contingencies Fund, therefore escaping even the rudimentary scrutiny exercised over the regular budget.

In terms of accountability to select committees, the Defence Committee is appointed by the House of Commons to examine the expenditure, administration, and policy of the MoD and associated bodies. However, a look at the Committee's agenda shows that it not only reviews the MoD and its activities, but that it also plays a major role in shaping defence policy. Recently, for example, the Committee has taken the lead on how the MoD can support the development of AI capacity and expertise in defence, and how defence can successfully be conducted in the grey zone of cyber-attacks and misinformation campaigns. In terms of accountability, the Committee goes further than just scrutinising the actions of the MoD. An example is the Committee's critical review of the (mis)treatment of women in the armed forces, which has revealed many systemic problems including sexual abuse and the failure by the armed forces to take adequate measures to prevent such abuse, or to provide redress for the victims.[45]

In contrast to the Defence Committee's relatively robust interpretation of its role as a mechanism of accountability for the MoD and the armed forces, a lighter touch appears to be taken to the security services. The Home Affairs Select Committee has largely failed to scrutinise the work of MI5 despite a number of attempts to engage with the director general. This is symptomatic of the broader 'convention which prevents matters relating to security and intelligence from being placed before Parliament'.[46]

One reason for excluding the Home Affairs Committee from scrutinising the secret service is that review of the intelligence services is meant to be undertaken by the Intelligence and Security Committee (ISC). This has been described as 'a most curious committee',[47] and one that is more deferential to the secret services than a fully-fledged select committee would be. Unlike select committees, the ISC is a statutory creation, originally by virtue of the Intelligence Services Act 1994, and now by the Justice and Security Act 2013, and having the job of overseeing the expenditure, administration, and operations of the three main security services.

It might be speculated that the government effectively nipped in the bud any attempts for full political scrutiny and accountability of the security services by the Home Affairs Committee, by creating a weaker version where evidence is given in private. The government 'continues to have greater control of the ISC than over other select committees', for example, by both the prime minister and home secretary having vetoes over certain matters being discussed by the ISC. Furthermore, its annual reports are 'badly disfigured by redaction, to the point of futility on some issues', though it has produced critical reports on the role of British agents in the detention of British nationals in Guantanamo Bay, and on the role of such agents in the detention and rendition of terrorist suspects to the US.[48]

The ISC's 2023 Report on International Partnerships reflects the difficulties the Committee encounters in trying to exercise effective scrutiny. As well as the 'Five Eyes alliance' with Australia, Canada, New Zealand, and the US, the UK has a unique intelligence-sharing partnership with the US, particularly between GCHQ and the US National Security Agency. Reviewing the role of these partnerships shows the Committee has some teeth, but not that many. The net result is often underwhelming.

In its 2023 Report, the Committee remarks that the

heads of the intelligence agencies had wanted the ISC to significantly reduce the scope of its inquiry into their relationships with foreign intelligence agencies. The Committee was stinging in its rebuke to the spy chiefs: 'the provision of information to the ISC ... is not a matter for negotiation, it is a statutory obligation' on the intelligence agencies 'and must be met if public and parliamentary confidence in the activities of the intelligence agencies is to be maintained'.[49]

Having established the ground rules, though, the Report remains so riddled with redaction that in the end we have to trust the Committee's rather bland conclusion that the 'UK's legal and compliance framework governing engagement in international partnerships is comprehensive'. We might also be encouraged by the ISC's finding that the 'importance of adhering to legal obligations seems to have been embedded into the operational culture and decision making of the agencies'. This 'cultural change' was welcomed by the ISC, especially when considering the 'problematic' history of the agencies' 'work with partners on detainee issues'. Even so, the ISC still recommended further improvement by the embedding of legal and compliance teams within operational missions, 'particularly in overseas hubs where detainee work with partners is central'.[50]

Worryingly, given the discrepancy between the US and UK in terms of intelligence capabilities, the ISC states that it is important 'that the UK retains sovereign intelligence capabilities to enable it to stand on its own two feet in intelligence terms, in the highly unlikely and undesirable event that there is a breakdown in the US partnership'.[51] The 'special relationship' with the US is reflected in the intimate and uneven relationship between GCHQ and the National Security Agency of the US. The ISC's report that UK actions under this partnership are at least more legally compliant than they used to be provides us with some crumbs of comfort.

Daniella Lock analyses that adoption of recent national security legislation and identifies that the government emphasises scrutiny by the ISC but only when seeking new national security powers. The executive then obstructs the ISC's work once those laws are on the books. Lock's conclusion is damning: 'the ISC is the only Parliamentary body procedurally equipped to conduct basic scrutiny of how the executive is exercising its national security powers. In its not being able to review such powers, Parliament is left in the dark and unable to scrutinise the operation of a collection of the executive's most secretive and invasive statutory powers'.[52] The undermining of both judicial and democratic accountability means that national security powers are either 'less regulated or, in some cases, unregulated'.[53]

4

Great Power Status

As well as the domestic constitution, the UK, as a sovereign state, is also subject to a complex international constitution, which also contains a combination of legal and political elements. As might be expected, defence and security are fundamental to the international constitution. This is due to strong evidence that we live in a very violent world. There are numerous armed conflicts being fought, tens of thousands of weapons of mass destruction (WMDs) in existence, and trillions of dollars are spent annually by states on military establishments. The UK has a powerful defence industry, with companies like BAE Systems playing a key role, as well as a private security industry with companies like G4S having global reach. Arms production and their export/import are seen as important aspects of state sovereignty, and the UK is comfortably amongst the top ten countries in terms of arms exports.

Looking at this evidence from a viewpoint outside Planet Earth, an alien would probably conclude that humankind is bent on self-destruction. However, the instinct for survival, inherent in human nature, provides a restraint on the use of these means of violence, though that restraint appears to be under increasing stress with the growth in existential conflicts and grandiose claims to territorial expansion.

In order to ensure the survival of the planet, more specifically the system of international relations based on nation-states, governments and other key players act to establish the basic conditions for the control of violence. Without controlling and containing violence in international relations, it would not be possible to establish a viable international political and legal order. Overall, the aim of international law in the field of defence and security is to reduce the levels of violence between states and, in the human rights era, against civilian populations, by addressing existential threats to states, peoples, and groups.

The security hierarchy

In line with the practice of many sovereign states, the UK has developed a significant defence capability. Unlike most other states the UK's armoury includes the possession of nuclear weapons. All sovereign states, whatever their levels of militarisation, come within the international constitution, whose primary function is to ensure international peace and security. The international constitution gives the UK rights but also imposes duties towards other states in the field of defence and security. These rights and duties are found in treaties, some of which purport to be constitutional (for example, the

UN Charter 1945). Other treaties are lawmaking (for example, the Nuclear Non-Proliferation Treaty 1968), contractual (for example, the North Atlantic Treaty 1949), political (for example, the Helsinki Final Act 1975, establishing what later became the Organisation for Security and Co-operation in Europe, or OSCE), or informal, for example in the so-called special relationship between the UK and US.

The international constitution also binds the UK into international organisations such as the UN, NATO, OSCE, and, until 2020, the EU. Organisations exercise defence and security powers on the international plane, ranging from peace initiatives to sanctions and the authorisation of collective military action. All of these collective actions rely on contributions (financial, political, and military) by member states.

The opening words of the UN Charter echo those of the US Constitution with the phrase 'we the peoples of the United Nations', which then continues: 'determined to save succeeding generations from the scourge of war, which twice in our lifetime has brought untold sorrow to mankind'. The world order embodied by the UN Charter was seen in constitutional terms by US President Truman at the formal adoption of the Charter in 1945, when he declared that: 'this Charter, like our own Constitution, will be expanded and improved as time goes on'.[1] Constitutions contain broad phrases that can develop over time, through practice and interpretation, and the UN Charter very much fits that mould. To its grand purposes of peace and security, human rights, self-determination, and economic prosperity, others have been added such as protecting the environment while pursuing sustainable development.

The UN is a universal organisation of 193 member states that sit as sovereign equals (at least in terms of voting rights) in the General Assembly. However, primary responsibility for the maintenance of international peace and security is given to the UN Security Council, the smaller executive-type organ of fifteen member states, where five states have permanent membership (China, Russia, France, the US, and the UK – known as the P5) each with the right to veto any proposed resolution beyond the innocuous. Decisions on key UN actions, ranging from peace plans to sanctions and military actions, have to receive the support of all five permanent members – or at least have to avoid the veto of one or more of those countries.

In reality the US, USSR, and UK shaped the UN around the Security Council and offered it on a take-it-or-leave-it basis to the rest of the world – at the time less than fifty states, which did not include colonised and defeated states. As the smaller states were so dependent upon the US in the bleak economic aftermath of the Second World War, they had to accept what the *New York Times* termed at the time a 'virtual world dictatorship' by the victorious allies.

The Security Council is empowered by the Charter not only to make recommendations for peaceful resolution of disputes and conflicts (under Chapter VI), but also to take action in the shape of coercive measures such as sanctions and military enforcement action (under Chapter VII). When the geopolitical context is favourable, and consensus can be achieved amongst the P5, executive actions to tackle threats to international peace have been taken, probably most impressively in response to Iraq's invasion of Kuwait in 1990. The Council imposed comprehensive and enforced sanctions against Iraq, binding upon all states, and ultimately authorised the use of force against Iraq by a US-led coalition of over fifty willing states by virtue of Resolution 678 of 1990. President George Bush declared that this action embodied a new world order of cooperation. It was brief, but for a period in the early 1990s, the UN was proactive in supporting the growth of democracy and human rights. However, that post-Cold War honeymoon period was brought to an abrupt end by the failures of the US/UN in Somalia in 1993, and driven home by the ineptitude of the UN and member states in the face of the genocide in Rwanda in 1994.

The Security Council has also developed its powers through practice and innovative interpretations of what measures are necessary to maintain international peace and security, for example through the creation of international criminal tribunals for the former Yugoslavia and Rwanda. These courts tried political and military leaders for atrocities committed in those countries during the mid-1990s. After 9/11, the Council also adopted a resolution requiring states to adopt measures to tackle terrorism that, controversially, appeared to be a form of binding international legislation.[2]

The Security Council has also co-opted a power first exercised by the UN General Assembly in 1956 in response to the Suez Crisis, to create 'blue-helmeted' peacekeeping forces. The functions of such forces have expanded from their original purpose as buffer forces between states that have agreed to stop fighting, towards more aggressive stabilisation forces within states (for example, in the DR Congo) where the aim is to prop up the government and help it establish sovereign authority over lawless areas of the country.

There is a convention that the troops of permanent members are not involved in peacekeeping, meaning that forces are in effect created by the P5, operating through the Security Council, and carried out by the militaries of developing countries. There are exceptions to this convention; for example, the UK has been the lead state in the buffer force that has been on the divided island of Cyprus since 1964, not long after the UK withdrew as the colonial power in 1960. Although the UN is in command of UN peacekeeping forces, the reality is that the British contingent, as with others, is under the effective control of its own commanders and subject to national military law.[3]

As well as military enforcement and peacekeeping measures, the UN Security Council is empowered to impose economic sanctions on states, such as the ones imposed on Iraq for its invasion of Kuwait in 1990. These sanctions badly hurt the civilian population, more so than the governing elite who benefitted from controlling the black market that emerged in the shadow of sanctions. Corruption grew around the sanctions, drawing in other countries and the UN itself.[4] In its practice after Iraq, the Security Council has pivoted towards smarter sanctions targeted at members of regime elites, armed groups, and terrorist organisations. Targeted sanctions have at times been challenged, with limited success, before national courts as infringing basic liberties.[5]

Sanctions have become part of the international landscape, being imposed not only by the UN Security Council but also by organisations such as the EU and an increasing number of states acting without any authority from any organisation. Sanctions have moved from being a power exercised collectively through organisations to tackle threats to international peace, to being claimed as a right belonging to individual states acting unilaterally on the basis of a perceived threat to that country. Following extensive US practice, the UK is one of the small number of states claiming a right to impose sanctions unilaterally, having adopted a statute empowering itself to do so in the light of its withdrawal from the EU.[6]

As a permanent member of the Security Council the UK has special privileges, in particular the right to veto or block Security Council decisions. The UK also shares responsibility with the other fourteen members of the

Security Council, particularly the other four permanent members, for upholding the UN's primary purpose of maintaining peace and security. However, the national self-interest of each of the P5 often prevents any executive action. A permanent member will often cynically cast its vote to protect itself or its allies, for example the US in the case of Israel. UK Prime Minister Tony Blair criticised the 'unreasonable' threat of vetoes by Russia and France in 2003 when he was arguing for a further resolution authorising the use of force against Iraq because of its alleged failure to disarm. However, the UK did not argue that the veto should, in certain cases, be ignored, nor has it sacrificed its own veto power or circumscribed it to any real extent. The UK has exercised its veto to block resolutions under Chapter VI, for example in the case of Suez in 1956, when the Charter legally requires that, as a party to a dispute, it should have abstained from voting.[7]

There have been attempts to limit the veto, for instance through a non-binding convention of 2015, which aimed to create an expectation that permanent members would refrain from using the veto to prevent appropriate action by the Security Council to address genocide, crimes against humanity, or war crimes (collectively known as core crimes).[8] Further, this was meant to reinforce the emergence of a responsibility to protect, or R2P, in the case of core crimes being committed within or by a state unwilling or unable to prevent them.[9]

A strong argument can be made that the UN ought

to act to prevent genocide, crimes against humanity, and other egregious violations of human rights, either because there is a duty on states and organisations to act within their legal competences to prevent such violations of international law,[10] or simply because such actions inherently undermine peace and security. The only clear legitimate security community that is empowered to react by authorising military action in such circumstances is the UN Security Council. But, the Security Council's *discretionary* power to deal with threats to the peace under Chapter VII is difficult to reconcile with a legal *responsibility* to protect civilian populations.

This partly explains the different reactions of the Security Council to Libya and Syria when crimes against humanity were being committed in both. Of course, it is easier to criticise the Security Council for failing to act in the case of Syria when it acted so decisively to authorise the use of force, primarily by the UK and France, against Libya in 2011.[11] However, the different perceptions of the threat within the permanent membership disabled it from acting to try to prevent core crimes being committed with appalling regularity in Syria.

The obvious weakness in placing the burden of responsibility to respond to core crimes on a body in which a veto by any permanent member can block any effective action leads to the question of whether there are alternative legitimate and lawful configurations of states that can fulfil R2P on behalf of the international community. In other words, when the Security Council is deadlocked in the face of imminent and catastrophic violence then the argument is that other organisations, groups of states, or indeed states acting unilaterally, should be able to act to authorise necessary measures to stop the atrocities and prevent further violence. As yet, there is no agreement amongst states that action can be taken outside of the Security Council, though the UK has in practice justified certain uses of force on these grounds.

The nuclear hierarchy

The security hierarchy, whereby five states possess great power status within the UN, has been bolstered by the nuclear hierarchy, which was developed separately from the UN Charter. It was formalised by the Nuclear Non-Proliferation Treaty (NPT) in 1968. Nuclear weapons were first used in August 1945 by the US against the Japanese cities of Hiroshima and Nagasaki. This was after the UN Charter had been adopted in June 1945. The secrecy surrounding the development of such weapons by the US meant that there was no reference to them in the Charter. Despite this attempt at secrecy, the Soviet Union had the bomb by 1949.

The UK government decided that it should build a nuclear bomb in 1947, the argument being won by Foreign Secretary Ernest Bevin, who stated that: 'we could not afford to acquiesce in an American monopoly of this new development'. The 'central aim' of UK strategy was 'to convince the Soviet leadership that – even without the Americans – the British could mount an unacceptably destructive blow to them'.[12] The UK tested its first atomic weapon in October 1952 in Australia, and a thermonuclear warhead ('Yellow Sun') off Christmas Island in 1957. In 1963, the UK, along with the US and USSR, became parties to the Partial Test Ban Treaty of 1963, which was seen as a way of slowing down the nuclear arms race, though it did not prohibit underground testing.[13]

British service veterans who witnessed these tests in the period 1952–67, along with aboriginal people in parts of Australia where nuclear tests took place, lost a case for compensation against the British government in 2012. The claimants had argued that the MoD was aware it was exposing them to harmful levels of radiation – indeed treated them like 'lab-rats'. The Supreme Court dismissed the case on the basis that the claimants were out of time.[14] The MoD had, prior to this, adopted an attitude which forced veterans into proving causation while denying them access to secret files. This is in contrast to other countries such as the US, where compensation for test veterans is the norm.

With France testing the bomb in 1960 and China in 1964, the five nuclear weapons states wanted to prevent the further proliferation of nuclear weapons, stopping their spread to other states while keeping their own privileged status. This was achieved by the NPT of 1968, supported by the work of the International Atomic Energy Agency (IAEA). Under the 'grand bargain', as the NPT is sometimes known, the nuclear hierarchy was embodied in international law. Those states already possessing nuclear weapons by 1968 were legally allowed to keep them, while no other state party to the treaty was permitted to develop them.

As with the UN Charter's centralisation of power in the P5, the NPT incorporates a similar sovereign inequality. As such, the UK has privileges belonging to the same five states that are permanent members of the Security Council, namely the right to possess nuclear weapons. However, it also has legal duties along with the other nuclear weapons states – to negotiate to achieve nuclear disarmament as required by Article VI of the NPT.

Arguably too, the recognised nuclear weapons states have the responsibility to prevent nuclear war, although this comes from the shared political view of those states that the balance of nuclear weaponry across the globe provides a stabilising deterrent on their use and, more broadly, on ruptures to peace and security. As stated by Rodric Brathwaite: 'mutual deterrence is a delicate thing. It works because both sides terrify themselves and one another into avoiding war'.[15] The vast majority of states were persuaded to join the NPT and accept its unequal treatment with promises of security guarantees whereby nuclear umbrellas were extended to allies of the nuclear weapons states, as well as with promises of the transfer of peaceful nuclear technology to developing states and the long-term prospect of nuclear disarmament.

In 1996, when the International Court of Justice was asked by the UN General Assembly for an advisory opinion on the legality of the use of nuclear weapons, the Court baulked at the task and decided, by a bare majority, that it was unclear whether the use of nuclear weapons was lawful or unlawful in situations when 'the very survival of the state was at stake'.[16] The UK had strongly argued that the use of nuclear weapons was lawful in self-defence and under humanitarian law in circumstances where the military advantage outweighed civilian losses.

In 2014, the UK again escaped censure by the ICJ for its continued retention of nuclear weapons despite the obligation to negotiate to disarm in the NPT. This was in a case brought against it (and other nuclear weapons states) by the Marshall Islands. This was a country where US nuclear weapons tests had been carried out when it was under the trusteeship of the US. The Court, again by the barest majority, dismissed the cases on very narrow, legalistic grounds, thereby saving the nuclear weapons states from embarrassment.[17] Judge Bedjaoui, in a passionate dissent, pointed out that the international community as a whole was the loser in the Court's decision to dismiss the case, saying that: 'since one sad morning in August 1945, nuclear weapons, an insane means of mass destruction, has left the human race living under a death sentence'.

Dissatisfaction with the commitment of the great powers to nuclear disarmament under the NPT led to a significant number of non-nuclear weapons states adopting the Treaty on the Prohibition of Nuclear Weapons

2017. The rupture in the international governance of nuclear weapons is further reflected not only by the failure to prevent proliferation to Israel, North Korea, India, and Pakistan, but also by the increased threats from the great powers to make use of nuclear weapons, principally by President Putin of Russia during the conflict in Ukraine.

Since 1969, under 'Operation Relentless', the Royal Navy has undertaken the task of providing the UK's nuclear deterrent through the deployment of up to four submarines equipped with missiles carrying nuclear warheads. Currently, the UK has four Vanguard-class nuclear-powered submarines, with at least one submarine being on active service at any one time, each one carrying up to eight Trident missiles with forty nuclear warheads.[18] Each warhead is capable of destroying a city.

In the 2016 parliamentary debates on the replacement of Vanguard with new Dreadnought submarines to carry Trident missiles, the House of Commons supported the government's assessment that the UK's independent minimum credible nuclear deterrent, based on a continuous at-sea deterrence posture, would remain essential 'to deter the most extreme threats to the UK's national security and way of life and that of the UK's allies'. The House of Commons, by a significant majority, voted in support of the government's decision to replace the current nuclear submarines, recognising the importance of this for the UK's defence industrial base and in supporting thousands of highly skilled engineering jobs. Parliament also stated that the UK 'remains committed to reducing its overall nuclear weapon stockpile by the mid-2020s'; and supported the government's commitment to work 'towards a safer and more stable world, pressing for key steps towards multilateral disarmament'.[19] Despite this commitment, in 2021 the UK reversed any reduction in warheads with a promise to increase their number from 225 to 260 in the light of the 'prevailing security environment'.[20] This was before the increased nuclear threat from Russia had fully materialised after its invasion of Ukraine in 2022. This invasion also led to a debate about the role of NATO.

NATO as a security organisation?

It might be understood that, when the UK is fighting alongside its allies against a common enemy, the use of force by the UK must be both just and lawful, harking back to the colossal efforts of the Allies during the Second World War. Those Allies formed the core of the permanent membership of the UN Security Council. However, the ideal of great power unity collectively fighting aggression was quickly lost. In 1946, Winston Churchill spoke about an 'iron curtain' descending across Europe, signalling the beginning of the Cold War. In 1948, the Berlin blockade, the communist coup in Czechoslovakia, and the lack of unity in the permanent membership of the UN Security Council, led Western powers to create NATO to defend Western Europe and North America. The preamble to the Washington or North Atlantic

Treaty of 1949 declared that the state parties were 'determined to safeguard the freedom, common heritage and civilisation of their peoples, founded on the principles of democracy, individual liberty and the rule of law'.

In appearance, at least, the North Atlantic Treaty is a form of international contract between those thirty-two states party to the treaty. NATO, at least at its inception, was a defence pact rather than a security organisation. In Article 5, each NATO state promises to come to the aid of an attacked NATO state in exchange for the promises of other state parties to come to its defence if attacked. However, the UK sometimes seems to waver in this commitment, at one point stating that Article 5 does not create a legal 'obligation' to come to the defence of other attacked state parties since Article 5 only commits each party to take action 'as it deems necessary'.[21] However, Russia's attack on a non-NATO member state – Ukraine – in 2022 has seemingly led to a hardening in attitude towards the commitment under Article 5 of the NATO Treaty. The question of Ukraine's possible future membership of NATO – vehemently opposed by President Putin of Russia – also shows the hardening of the security guarantees that come with NATO membership. If Ukraine is allowed to join NATO, member states will have to defend it, potentially pitting US and Russian forces against each other for the first time and making World War Three that much closer. This could all change, as the second term of US President Trump shows a profound disdain for Europe and NATO.

The type of attack envisaged by the NATO treaty was by one state or group of states against another, principally by the Soviet Union and its allies (forming the Warsaw Pact in 1955) against the United States and its allies. However, the first time Article 5 of the NATO Treaty was invoked by the North Atlantic Council was on 12 September 2001, after the 9/11 terrorist attacks on the United States, when planes hijacked by al-Qaeda terrorists flew into the World Trade Center and the Pentagon.

In October 2001, in response to the attacks of 9/11 and stated to be in self-defence under international law, the US used force in Afghanistan with UK support to destroy al-Qaeda bases but also to remove the Taliban regime that had provided a safe haven for the terrorist organisation. Prime Minister Tony Blair justified British involvement as not simply a 'just cause, though this cause is just. It is to protect our country, our people, ... our way of life'. He went on to say that 'if attacked, we will respond. We will defend ourselves ... We will see this struggle to the end and to the victory that would mark the victory not of revenge but of justice over the evil of terrorism'.[22] The UK formally justified its action in Afghanistan in terms of collective self-defence, in other words the UK was coming to the defence of the victim state – the US – even though the US was clearly capable of defending itself. It may be for this reason that Prime Minister Blair portrayed the attack of 9/11 as an attack on the UK as well as the US. Sixty-seven UK citizens were among the 2,977 who were killed by the attacks.

Informally, the so-called 'special relationship', a term coined by Winston Churchill in 1946, between the US and the UK has led the UK to fight alongside the US in a number of conflicts in addition to Afghanistan in 2001. In some ways this relationship seems more important than NATO, at least in terms of the deployment of British forces alongside US forces. For example, in the Korean War of 1950 and the invasion of Iraq in 2003, UK troops were deployed to fight alongside of US forces to enforce UN resolutions, though only the Korean conflict was backed by a clear Security Council resolution authorising the use of force.

The UK does not always follow the US into battle; most notably the government of Harold Wilson refused to deploy UK troops to the ill-fated Vietnam War in which the US became directly involved from 1965 to 1973. However, there is a sharing of intelligence as well as enhanced security and defence working arrangements between the US and UK, in addition to an integrated nuclear strategy. The latter is underpinned by a formal treaty – the Mutual Defence Agreement of 1954, which has been renewed on a number of occasions and extended indefinitely in 2024. There are also US military bases in the UK, as well as a UK–US Diego Garcia base in the Chagos Islands. In 2025, the UK announced that it had agreed with Mauritius for the return of the Chagos Islands but that it had also agreed a ninety-nine-year lease for the continued use of the base. It seems there is something tangible in the special relationship, especially in the area of defence and security, but the traction that it might have very much depends on the closeness of the relationship struck between the US president and British prime minister.

As a leading member of NATO, the UK has tried reformulate the purposes of the organisation through practice. First, it might claim that after Afghanistan in 2001, the right of self-defence has been understood to include coming to the aid of a NATO member if they have been attacked by terrorist organisations as well as by states. Secondly, the UK contends that military action can be taken through NATO to prevent major atrocities as was the case in the NATO bombing campaign over Kosovo in 1999. In effect, this amounted to a claim that NATO has the legitimacy and authority to act when the UN Security Council is deadlocked, in effect to act as an alternative security organisation. This is neither what the North Atlantic Treaty envisaged nor what the UN Charter allows.[23] As I argue below, this is just one example of the UK being a lawbreaker, though it might claim that it is breaking an old (bad) law to make a new (good) law.

Lawbreaker or lawmaker?

Since 1945, the UK has shown itself to be one of the most active countries in terms of deploying its armed forces overseas. The UK has a track record of relying on controversial legal justifications for its military interventions. While the UN Charter prohibits the threat or use of force by states, it does allow for self-defence from armed attacks as well as military enforcement action taken under UN Security Council authority. For instance, the UK government relied on self-defence when the Falklands Islands were attacked by Argentina in 1982. In sending troops to the US-led actions in Korea in 1950 and Iraq in 1991, or joining France in bombing Libya in 2011, the UK could legitimately claim that it had authority to do so from the UN Security Council in the form of a clear resolution authorising willing states to undertake 'necessary measures' (recognised UN-speak for the use of force). In other instances, the UK government has either strained to apply these exceptions or has gone beyond the international constitutional framework to argue for controversial customary rights to use force.

An instance of the UK's continuing post-1945 belief in itself as a global imperial power was its military intervention in Suez in 1956 alongside France to protect British and French interests there. Here, the UK had crossed the Rubicon with even the US refusing to support it. Politically and legally Suez was a disaster. Prime Minister Anthony Eden 'was aware that he was coming perilously close to the limits of what a statesman in a democracy can do'.[24] Eden reputedly complained about the government's law officers' advice against intervention: 'lawyers are always against our doing anything. For God's sake keep them out of it. This is a political affair'.[25]

Sometimes the use of force has weak legal justification but stronger claims to be morally justified. The NATO bombing campaign of 1999, in which the UK played a prominent role, was aimed at protecting the people of Kosovo from Serb forces. It did not have the authority of the Security Council, as was claimed by the UK, and the right of humanitarian intervention also put forward by the government as a legal justification is only consistently claimed by the UK as a customary right in the modern era. The claims and actions of one state do not make customary international law.

In its review of the Kosovo bombing campaign, the Foreign Affairs Committee concluded that 'NATO's military action, if of dubious legality in the current state of international law, was justified on moral grounds'.[26] Despite this, the UK government continues to fall back on the claimed right of humanitarian intervention. The RAF airstrikes against Syria in April 2018 were undertaken in response to the use of chemical weapons by the Assad regime. The airstrikes had the hallmarks of a punitive attack against Syria for a violation of international law, though the UK government justified it as a use of force to prevent humanitarian suffering.[27]

The 2003 US–UK invasion of Iraq was possibly the most controversial British post-1945 military intervention. It was based on the alleged failure by Iraq to fully give up its WMD. The legal justification was a novel and unconvincing argument that the failure by Iraq to fully comply with the disarmament obligations imposed by the Security Council at the end of the war in 1991 led to a revival of the Security Council resolution of 1990 that had authorised the use of force against Iraq.[28] This 'revival' argument, as it came to be known, was cobbled together as a new resolution authorising force against Iraq in 2003 and was not accepted due to objections from France as well as Russia. The attorney general's apparent confidence in this legal argument was sufficient to help convince MPs of the legality of the use of force against Iraq and so,[29] with US–UK forces ready to invade Iraq, they voted in support of it. However, the attorney general's unadulterated legal opinion, revealed much later, was equivocal and leaned against the 'revival' argument towards the need for a new authorising resolution.[30]

The 'revival' argument was not only disingenuous in the circumstances of Iraq in 2003, when the evidence of Saddam's hidden WMDs was 'sexed up' by both the US and UK,[31] but it also has potentially unintended consequences. For example, could a state claim to be able to use force against North Korea in the current era on the basis that its regular violations of the armistice agreement that brought the war to a 'temporary' end in 1953 can revive a Security Council resolution of 1950, which had recommended the use of force by a US-led coalition to repel North Korean aggression against South Korea?[32] The resolutions on Korea and Iraq were instances of the Security Council making executive decisions aimed at tackling immediate threats; they were not pieces of legislation that somehow endure until they are repealed.

As well as unsustainable arguments based on Security Council resolutions, the UK is not averse to abusing, or at least over-claiming, its right of self-defence under international law in order to provide sufficient legal cover for its military interventions. In justifying the use of armed force against the Houthis in Yemen in January 2024, the government claimed to be acting in self-defence in response to drone and missile strikes aimed at shipping, including warships, in the Red Sea.[33] While the shooting down of drones and missiles heading towards such shipping is clearly within the right of self-defence, the strikes within Yemen meant to reduce Houthi capacity seem akin to law enforcement operations, which might explain why the US and UK sought further justification in a Security Council resolution. However, that resolution affirmed the right of states to defend their vessels from attacks. It did not authorise more extensive military enforcement action in Yemen.[34]

Controversial wars raise questions about the legal liabilities of the government (the state) as well as political and military leaders. It may also lead to some service personnel questioning their duty to obey orders to deploy to what they might consider to be an aggressive, or otherwise illegal, war. Examples of service personnel refusing to deploy to Iraq from 2003 onwards were met with the full force of military justice and convictions by court martial for refusal to obey lawful orders. The concern for ordinary soldiers is whether the order to deploy is lawfully made under UK law, which they were. According to the courts, issues of international law, at least at the initial stage of going to war, are for the government and those that made the decision to go to war.[35] Although the UK has accepted the jurisdiction of the International Criminal Court (ICC) as regards war crimes, crimes against humanity, and genocide, it has chosen not to be subject to the ICC as regards the crime of aggression, thereby precluding prosecution of those that made decisions to go to war.

Furthermore, for a case to be brought against a state before the International Court of Justice (ICJ) by another state it has to be demonstrated that both states have given consent.[36] A rare instance of the UK accepting the jurisdiction of the ICJ was the *Corfu Channel* case of 1949, when the UK brought a claim against Albania after its warship had suffered damage and loss of life from colliding with unmarked mines.[37] While the Court found for the UK on the claim (and unusually awarded it damages), it also found that the Royal Navy's response in sending a flotilla through the Channel to clear further mines was an unlawful intervention in Albania. The UK government's argument that its actions in the Corfu Channel were a form of law enforcement was roundly dismissed by the ICJ.

It was not until 1996 that the Albanian government paid damages to the UK for the loss of life and destruction of the warship. The wheels of international justice turn slowly, if they turn at all. Indeed, the only real judicial inroads into the power of the state to wage war with impunity have been made by the ECtHR which, on a relatively few occasions discussed in Chapter 2, has found the UK responsible for violations of the right to life and freedom from abuse during its military operations in Iraq.

There is a great deal of smoke and mirrors surrounding government decisions to go to war. It always claims to have international law on its side, when Suez, Kosovo, Iraq, and other uses of force show the legal basis is much less certain. But with courts and international bodies unable or unwilling to review the legal justifications given by the government, we return to the question of whether a political body like the House of Commons can play a role in holding the government to account under international law. In order to do this, an understanding of the debates surrounding the meaning of the rules of international law is needed.

The contours and parameters of even the most basic rules of international law are contested and subject to interpretation through practice. The rules state that force between states is prohibited, but the UN Charter allows for two exceptions: self-defence in the case of an armed attack and action taken under the authority of the UN Security Council for the maintenance or restoration of international peace and security. These rules are replete with ambiguity. What is 'force'? Does an imminent armed attack trigger the right of self-defence? When is an attack 'imminent'? What constitutes an authorisation from the Security Council? What if a veto blocks a resolution authorising an otherwise legitimate use of force (for example, to protect the civilian population of a state from core crimes being committed against them) – can states go ahead and use force or should they seek the authority of the UN General Assembly or a regional organisation?

These are just some of the questions that well-informed members of Parliament would have to consider when being asked to support the government's decision to go to war. These legal questions would have to be weighed alongside arguments raising humanitarian, ethical, and national and international security considerations. Given that MPs are not judges, they are better placed, in a democratic sense at least, to balance legal, political, and contextual considerations. However, this is dependent upon MPs being given sufficient information, in particular a full and balanced legal opinion. At the moment, the attorney general presents sanitised, black-and-white, summarised legal opinions, which disguise any controversy or ambiguity – a short-term expedient measure that can have long-term negative repercussions.

5

Conclusion

Towards efficiency and democracy in defence
The importance of defence to the UK is not reflected in the constitutional frameworks that should serve to limit the exercise of excessive or arbitrary powers by the government (and its agents) in the name of defence and security. The defence paradox – the mismatch between the centrality of defence to the UK and the lack of constitutional restraints upon it – can only be addressed by a rebalancing of the underlying constitutional values of efficiency and democracy, as well as the legal and political elements of both national and international constitutions.

The dominance of executive or governmental power at both national and international levels means that there is very little legal or, indeed, political accountability. Arguments of efficiency – that the executive needs to act quickly, effectively, and increasingly secretively – overpower arguments of democracy. The dominant voice of political and military leaders is that we simply can't afford to delay crucial decisions on national security by political debate in Parliament or lengthy court cases.

Of course, if the UK were under imminent attack, then the state has to act quickly to defend itself and its people, and issues of accountability for its actions must come later. However, many modern uses of force are matters of judgement or choice. Did the UK need to invade Iraq in 2003? Was the UK defending itself from attack when it sent troops to Afghanistan in 2001? Did the US need the UK's assistance in these two wars? Was there a necessity of self-defence in the Suez Crisis in 1956 or even in the Falklands War in 1982? The US certainly did not think so in the latter two instances.

How could a better balance be achieved between the 'efficient' and 'democratic' parts of the constitution, as well as the 'legal' and 'political' elements? A start could be made by taming the war powers prerogative, with Parliament finally adopting a War Powers Resolution or War Powers Act. A further step would be to delimit excessive discretionary powers, whether statutory or prerogative. Where there are statutory frameworks (for example regarding the security services, civil contingencies, and the government's response to Covid-19), it is questionable whether they provide the right balance between efficiency and democratic accountability, as well as between the executive powers granted and the basic rights of individuals.

The legal constitution in defence and security favours the state over the individual. This needs to be rebalanced. Despite increased statutory provision, prerogative powers still permeate defence and security. Such powers are often presented as residual, but in practice their presence and use within the political constitution is so much more than that. They need to be regularised in law and subject to judicial review.

Accelerating the penetration of international laws into the UK constitution by, for example, the UK accepting that the International Criminal Court would, in the future, have authority over its leaders for the crime of aggression, would curtail the number of expeditionary (and often disastrous) wars engaged in by the UK government. Increasing the penetration of international laws into the national legal order could also be achieved by removing the secrecy surrounding the attorney general's full legal advice given to governments on proposed military actions.

The North Atlantic Treaty sorely needs updating to reflect changes in international security and the growth in both membership and purposes of the organisation. NATO should, however, remain within the broad parameters set for international peace and security in the UN Charter of 1945. The so-called 'special relationship' between the UK and US seems to mean that the UK is often the junior partner in expeditionary warfare primarily designed to further the American agenda. Such loose, non-binding, and one-sided relationships should be abandoned in favour of ones based on clear legal obligations.

The connection of defence to the international constitutional order should be reassessed by considering how the UK's privileged position could be used to enhance defence as a legally constituted and constrained concept. The UK government should take the lead on the disarmament of nuclear weapons. It should also take the lead in restricting the use of the veto in the UN Security Council and in arguing that the UN General Assembly can authorise measures when the Security Council is deadlocked by the veto. In these ways, the UK would reflect and justify its status as a great power on the international stage, not in a military sense, but legally and morally.

Notes

1. Framing Defence

1   A. V. Dicey, *Introduction to the Study of the Law of the Constitution* (London, 10th edn, 1959, originally published 1885), p. 91.

2   W. Bagehot, *The English Constitution* (Oxford, 2001, originally published 1867), pp. 10–22.

3   BBC News, 'SAS has golden pass to get away with murder, inquiry told', 8 January 2025.

4   BBC News, 'Shamima Begum loses final UK court bid over citizenship', 7 August 2024.

5   *Thoburn v Sunderland City Council* [2002] EWHC 195 (Admin).

6   House of Lords Select Committee on the Constitution, 'Reviewing the Constitution: Terms of Reference and Methods of Working', 1st Report, HL Paper 11, Session 2001–02, para. 20

7   H. M. Government, 'Global Britain in a Competitive Age: The Integrated Review of Security, Defence, Development and Foreign Policy' (CP 403, 2021), p. 13.

8   Dicey, *Introduction*, p. 424.

9   Ibid., p. 24.

10   Cabinet Manual (2011), para. 5.85

11 The Convention on the Prohibition of the Development, Production, Stockpiling and Use of Chemical Weapons and on their Destruction 1993.

12 R. Tully, 'UK Nuclear Modernisation is Crucial for US–UK Relations and NATO's Future', RUSI Commentary, 11 September 2024.

13 T. Tugendhat and L. Croft, 'The Fog of Law: An introduction to the legal erosion of British fighting power' (Policy Exchange Report, 2013).

14 E. de Vattel, *The Law of Nations, or the Principles of Natural Law, Applied to the Conduct and to the Affairs of Nations and of Sovereigns* (Indianapolis, 2008), p. 246.

15 https://www.gov.uk/government/organisations/ministry-of-defence/about#responsibilities-and-priorities

16 *Council of Civil Services Union v Minister for Civil Service* [1985] AC, p. 374 at p. 410.

17 *Attorney General v Tomline* [1880] 14 ChD, p. 66.

18 M. Radin, 'The Myth of the Magna Carta', *Harvard Law Review* 60 (1947), p. 1062.

19 Dicey, *Introduction*, p. 202.

20 J. A. G. Griffith, 'The Political Constitution', *Modern Law Review* (1979), p. 19.

21 *R (Gentle) v The Prime Minister* [2008] UKHL, p.10, para 24 (Lord Hope).

2. The Legal Constitution

1   A. W. Bradley, K. D. Ewing, and C. J. S. Knight, *Constitutional and Administrative Law* (London, 2022), p. 14.

2   *R (Miller) v Secretary of State for Exiting the European Union* [2017] UKSC 5.

3   *R v Halliday* [1917] AC 260 260 at 268–9.

4   *Liversidge v Anderson* [1942] AC 208.

5   D. French, *Army Empire & Cold War: The British Army and Military Policy 1945–1971* (Oxford, 2012), p. 82.

6   Hansard, HC, vol. 430, cols 42–4, 12 November 1946.

7   G. Rubin, *Murder, Mutiny and the Military: British Court Martial Cases 1940–1966* (London, 2005).

8   BBC News, 'Britain must train citizen army, military chief warns', 24 January 2024.

9   MoD, 'How Defence Works' (version 6.0, Sept 2020), p. 4.

10   MoD, 'Defence in a Competitive Age' (CP 411, 2021), p. 5.

11   M. Hastings, *Finest Years: Churchill as Warlord 1940–45* (London, 2010), p. 129.

12   MoD, 'How Defence Works' (version 6.0, Sept 2020), p. 7.

13   French, *Army, Empire & Cold War*, pp. 153–5.

14   R. Braithwaite, *Armageddon and Paranoia: The Nuclear Confrontation* (London, 2017), p. 202.

15   Defence Nuclear Organisation/MoD, 'The UK's nuclear deterrent: what you need to know', 19 February 2018.

16 *Privacy International v Foreign Secretary* [2021] EWCA Civ. 330.

17 Bradley, Ewing, and Knight, *Constitutional Law*, p. 593.

18 *R (Khan) v Foreign Secretary* [2015] EWCA Civ 24.

19 Lord Hutton, Report of the Inquiry into the Circumstances Surrounding the Death of Dr David Kelly (HC 247, 28 January 2004); Lord Butler, Review of Intelligence on Weapons of Mass Destruction (HC 898, 14 July 2004).

20 P. F. Scott, 'State threats, security, and democracy: the National Security Act 2023', *Legal Studies* (2024), p. 260.

21 P. F. Scott, *The National Security Constitution* (London, 2018), p. 4.

22 Bradley, Ewing, and Knight, *Constitutional Law*, p. 624.

23 For example, *Belhaj v DPP* [2018] UKSC 33.

24 'Report of the Detainee Inquiry', December 2013.

25 Scott, *The National Security Constitution*, p. 35.

26 *Ahmed v HM Treasury* [2010] UKSC 2.

27 *R v Gul* [2013] UKSC 64.

28 *R (Miranda) v Secretary of State for the Home Department* [2016] EWCA Civ 6.

29 *A and Others v UK,* App No 3455/05, 19 February 2009, para 181.

30 Terrorism Protection and Investigation Measures Act 2011. See, for example, *Home Secretary v AP* [2010] UKSC 24.

31 N. D. White, *Democracy Goes to War: British Military Deployments under International Law* (Oxford), pp. 252–4.

32 UN Security Council Resolution 83 (1950).

33 'Summary of the UK Government Legal Position: The legality of UK military action to target Houthi facilities in Yemen on 12 January 2024'.

34 UN Security Council Resolution 2722 (2024).

35 N. D. White, *Military Justice: The Rights and Duties of Soldiers and Government* (Cheltenham, 2022), pp. 135–7.

36 Statute of the International Court of Justice (1945), Article 36.

37 *Corfu Channel Case* (1949) ICJ Rep 4.

31 Covert Human Intelligence Sources (Criminal Conduct) Act 2021.

32 Bradley, Ewing, and Knight, *Constitutional Law*, p. 492.

33 *Privacy International v Secretary of State* [2021].

34 Bradley, Ewing, and Knight, *Constitutional Law*, pp. 495–9.

35 *R (Liberty) v Home Secretary* [2019] EWHC 2057.

36 D. Lock, 'An increasingly chameleonic executive in UK national security law' (2024) *Public Law*, p. 400.

37 *CND v The Prime Minister* [2002] EWCC 2777, para. 39.

38 Lock, 'UK national security law', p. 397.

39 *Keyu v Secretary of State for Foreign Affairs* [2015] UKSC 69.

40 Lord Saville, 'Report of the Bloody Sunday Inquiry' (2010), vol. 1, p. 100. See also Lord Widgery, 'Report of the Tribunal into the events on Sunday, 30th January 1972' (1972), p. 98.

41 *R (Gentle) v The Prime Minister* [2008] UKHL 20, para. 58.

42 R. Ekins, J. Morgan, and T. Tugendhat, 'Clearing the Fog of Law: Saving our Armed Forces from Defeat by Judicial Diktat' (Policy Exchange, 2015).

43 Moses LJ, 'Foreword' in T. Tugendhat and L. Croft, 'The Fog of Law: An introduction to the Legal Erosion of British Fighting Power' (Policy Exchange, 2013).

44 *Smith v Ministry of Defence* [2013] UKSC 41.

45 *Al-Skeini v UK* (2011) 53 EHRR 589.

46 Sir John Chilcot, 'The Report of the Iraq Inquiry' (2016), vol. II, section 14.1.

47 *Hassan v United Kingdom*, Appl No 2970/09, 16 September 2014; *Al-Waheed and Serdar Mohammed v Ministry of Defence* [2017] UKSC 2.

48 *Ireland v UK*, Appl No 5310/71, 18 January 1978.

49 *Al-Skeini v UK* (2011).

50 Sir William Gage, 'The Report of the Baha Mousa Inquiry', vol. III) HC 1452-III) 8 September 2011, paras. 238–51.

51 ICC OTP, 'Report on Preliminary Examination Activities', 5 December 2018, para 195.

52 Forces Net, 'MoD Paid Over £20m In Iraq War Compensation Claims', 13 June 2017.

53 Haddon-Cave LJ, 'Independent Inquiry Relating to Afghanistan', launched on 15 December 2022.

54 *R v Blackman* [2017] EWCA Crim 190.

55 Sir Richard Henriques, 'Report of the Henriques Review into the Framework, Processes and Skills that the Service Justice System Requires for Overseas Operations', 29 July 2021.

56 *McCann v UK,* Appl No 18984/91, 27 September 1995.

57 L. Doswald-Beck, *Human Rights in Times of Conflict and Terrorism* (Oxford, 2011), 165.

58 *McCann* (1995), para 212.

59 *Armani da Silva v UK*, Appl No 5878/08, 30 March 2016.

60 Manchester Arena Inquiry Volume 3: Radicalisation and Preventability, HC 1137, 2 March 2023, para 24.

61 See the Terrorism (Protection of Premises) Bill (also known as Martyn's Law) 2024.

3. The Political Constitution

1 B. Donagan, *War in England 1642–1649* (Oxford, 2010), pp. 8–9.

2 E. R. Fidell, *Military Justice: A Very Short Introduction* (Oxford, 2016), p. 1.

3 Dicey, *Introduction*, p. 287.

4 H. M. Bowman, 'Martial Law and the English Constitution', *Michigan Law Review* 15 (1916), p. 93 at p. 106.

5 *R v Nelson and Brand* (1867) Cockburn's Report 85.

6 M. Burleigh, *Small Wars, Far Away Places* (London, 2013), pp. 374–85.

7 F. Ledwidge, *Losing Small Wars* (London, 2011), p. 29.

8 S. Casey-Maslen and Sean Connolly, *Police Use of Force under International Law* (Cambridge, 2017), p. 23.

9 Bradley, Ewing, and Knight, *Constitutional Law*, p. 449.

10 Council of Europe, Parliamentary Assembly, Recommendation 1742, 11 April 2006.

11 P. Rowe, 'The Soldier as Citizen in Uniform: A Reappraisal', *New Zealand Armed Forces Review* 7 (2007), p. 1.

12 Casey-Maslen and Connolly, *Police Use of Force,* p. 21.

13 Reference under s48A of the Criminal Appeal (Northern Ireland) Act 1966 (No.1 of 1975) [1976] 2 All ER 937 at 948.

14 *R v Clegg* [1995] I All ER 334; *R v Clegg* [2000] NI 305.

15 Northern Ireland Troubles (Legacy and Reconciliation) Act 2023. BBC News, 'Mixed reaction to government's Legacy Act repeal from victims', 5 December 2024.

16 See, for example, *Kelly and Others v United Kingdom*, Appl No 30054/96, 4 May 2001.

17 M. Head and S. Mann, *Domestic Deployment of the Armed Forces: Military Powers, Law and Human Rights* (London, 2009), p. 91.

18 M. Head, 'Calling Out the Troops and the Civil Contingencies Act: Some Questions of Concern', *Public Law* (2010), p. 341.

19 Coronavirus Act (2020).

20 Head and Mann, *Domestic Deployment*, p. 91, citing C. Walker and J. Broderick, *The Civil Contingencies Act 2004: Risk, Resilience and the Law in the United Kingdom* (Oxford, 2006), p. 251.

21 *Campaign for Nuclear Disarmament v The Prime Minister of the United Kingdom* [2002] EWHC 2777.

22 *Council of Civil Service Unions v Minister for the Civil Service* [1985] AC 374.

23 M. Bennett, 'Parliamentary scrutiny of counter-terrorism targeted killings: democratic accountability challenges of, and for, the political constitution', *Public Law* (2024), p. 45 at p. 62.

24 Ibid, p. 62. *R (Miller) v Secretary of State for Exiting the European Union* [2017] UKSC 5 at p. 49.

25 S. Dietrich, H. Hummell and S. Marschall, 'Strengthening parliamentary war powers in Europe: lessons from 25 national parliaments' (DECAF Policy Paper no 27, 2008), pp. 11–12.

26 J. Strong, 'Did Theresa May kill the War Powers Convention? Comparing parliamentary debates on UK intervention in Syria in 2013 and 2018', *Parliamentary Affairs* 75 (2022), p. 403.

27 House of Commons Public Administration Committee, 'Taming the prerogative: Strengthening ministerial accountability to Parliament', HC 422, 16 March 2004.

28 Cabinet Manual (2011), para. 5.85.

29 N. D. White, 'Strengthening democratic control of UK war power in an age of remote and hybrid warfare' (Ceasefire Centre for Civilian Rights, 2024).

30 *Hansard*, HC, vol. 743, col. 577, 15 January 2024.

31 BBC News, 'Rishi Sunak faces call for MP vote on Houthi airstrikes', 12 January 2024.

32 *Hansard*, HC, vol. 743, col. 577, 15 January 2024.

33 Ibid, col. 581.

34 BBC News, 'Starmer denies backtracking on military action vote', 14 January 2024.

35 B. Renz, 'Russia and "hybrid warfare"', *Contemporary Politics* 22 (2016), p. 283.

36 T. McCormack, 'The emerging parliamentary convention on British military action and warfare by remote control', *RUSI Journal* 161 (2016), p. 22 at p. 24.

37 Ibid.

38 Ibid, p. 22.

39 House of Lords, House of Commons Joint Committee on Human Rights, 'The government's policy on the use of drones for targeted killing', Second Report of Session 2015–16, HL Paper 141, HC 574, 10 May 2016.

40 Bennett, 'Parliamentary scrutiny of counter-terrorism targeted killings', p. 68.

41 Ibid, p. 65.

42 White, 'Strengthening democratic control of UK war power'.

43 A. C. L. Davies, *Accountability: A Public Law Analysis of Government by Contract* (Oxford, 2001), p. 76.

44 Bradley, Ewing, and Knight, *Constitutional Law*, p. 23.

45 Defence Committee, 'Protecting those who protect us: Women in the Armed Forces from recruitment to civilian life', HC 154 (2021).

46 Bradley, Ewing, and Knight, *Constitutional Law*, p. 620.

47 Ibid, p. 621.

48 Ibid, p. 622.

49 HC 288 (2023) para. 13.

50 Ibid, p. 95.

51 Ibid, para. 248.

52 D. Lock, 'An increasingly chameleonic executive in UK national security law', *Public Law* (2024), p. 405.

53 Ibid.

4. Great Power Status

1   S. C. Schlesinger, *Act of Creation: The Founding of the United Nations* (Boulder, 2003), p. 289.

2   UN Security Council Resolution 1373 (2001).

3   *Nissan v Attorney General* [1970] AC 179.

4   Independent Inquiry Committee into the United Nations Oil-for-Food Programme (Volcker Inquiry), 7 September 2005.

5   *HM Treasury v Ahmed* [2010] UKSC 2.

6   Sanctions and Anti-Money Laundering Act 2018.

7   UN Charter 1945, Article 27(3).

8   UN General Assembly and Security Council, 'Code of conduct regarding Security Council action against genocide, crimes against humanity or war crimes, UN Doc A/70/621-S/2015/978, 14 December 2015.

9   UNGA Res 60/1 (2005) paras 138–9.

10 See J. Heieck, *A Duty to Prevent Genocide: Due Diligence Obligations Among the P5* (Cheltenham, 2018).

11 UN Security Council Resolution 1973 (2011).

12 Braithwaite, *Armageddon and Paranoia*, p. 193.

13 The Comprehensive Nuclear Test Ban Treaty of 1996 has been ratified by the UK but has not yet come into force.

14 *Ministry of Defence v AB and Others* [2012] UKSC 9.

15 Braithwaite, *Armageddon and Paranoia*, p. 315.

16 *Legality of the Threat or Use of Nuclear Weapons* (1996) ICJ Rep 226 at para. 97.

17 *Obligations Concerning Negotiations Relating to the Cessation of the Nuclear Arms Race and to Nuclear*

Disarmament (Marshall Islands v United Kingdom) (2016) ICJ Rep, p. 833.

18 MoD, 'The UK's nuclear deterrent: what you need to know', 28 March 2024.

19 Hansard, HC Debates, vol. 613, col. 559 (Theresa May), 18 July 2016, adopted by 472 votes to 117.

20 C. Mills, 'Nuclear weapons at a glance: the United Kingdom', House of Commons Library Research Briefing 9077, 1 August 2024, p. 11.

21 House of Lords Select Committee on the Constitution, 'Waging War: Parliament's Role and Responsibility', Volume I, 15th Report of Session 2005–06, HL Paper 236-I, 27 July 2006, para 24.

22 *Hansard,* HC Deb, vol. 372, col. 814, 8 October 2001.

23 UN Charter 1945, Article 53.

24 D. Carlton, *Britain and the Suez Crisis* (London, 1988), p. 59.

25 A. Nutting, *No End of a Lesson: The Story of Suez* (London, 1967), p. 95.

26 House of Commons Foreign Affairs Select Committee, 'Kosovo', Fourth Report 1999–2000, paras 124–44.

27 Syria action – UK government legal position', 14 April 2018.

28 UN Security Council Resolution 678 (1990).

29 Attorney General's Advice released on 17 March 2003 in *Hansard*, HL, vol. 646, WA2-3, 17 March 2003.

30 J. Chilcot, 'Report of the Iraq Inquiry: Executive Summary', HC 264, 6 July 2016, pp. 119–20.